How to make Fantasy and Medieval Dioramas

Will Kalif

Copyright © 2012 Will Kalif and Kalif Publishing

All rights reserved.

ISBN:1480230375
ISBN-13:978-1480230378

DEDICATION

As always this book is dedicated to the one.

CONTENTS

	Acknowledgments	i
	Introduction	2
1	Some Basics Before Beginning	4
2	Designing Your Diorama	9
3	Building Your Diorama	13
4	Trees, Water and Rocks	38
5	Electricity and Special Effects	64
6	Buildings and Structures	79
7	Painting Techniques	90
8	Unique Dioramas	93

ACKNOWLEDGMENTS

Special acknowledgment goes to Sophia Dotson for all the fantastic detail work she did on the medieval village diorama and to James Joaquim for all his help in sculpting, molding, casting, and painting the numerous walls that go around the medieval village.

Introduction

The art of making dioramas has changed dramatically over the past several years. It used to rest solely in the hands of model railroad enthusiasts and war buffs. The basic goal of these diorama makers was to showcase a train or a military model in a very realistic miniature scene that was appropriate for the model; a tank would become part of a crumbled war-torn village, or a train would be passing through a picturesque countryside. The scenes varied but the goal was always the same: Make the scene look as real as possible in a miniature scale.

And over the course of several decades these enthusiasts came up with a very wide variety of tool, tips, and techniques to achieve this realism.

In today's world, with the popularity of fantasy movies, books, role-playing games, tabletop wargaming and video games a whole new genre of diorama making has been born.

It is the genre of fantasy and medieval dioramas. No longer do diorama makers work with just trains or military vehicles.

They now have a very diverse host of figures, models, and items they can build into a diorama —a new kind of diorama. These items run the absolute gamut of fantasy imagination from Ogres, to Elves, Dragons, Castles, Battlegrounds, and just about any figure or world that can be imagined.

A New Definition of Realism

This new type of diorama, by definition changes the rules of diorama making and now the goal isn't to make the diorama landscape as realistic as possible by mimicking, in miniature, a real world place.

The goal is now to make the fantasy landscape look as realistic as possible in a way that makes sense for the miniatures or items that are being used or showcased in the scene.

This new goal gives diorama makers a lot of freedom to create fantastic looking scenes that exist nowhere else but in the builder's imagination.

And the beauty of this is that all of the old diorama making techniques are still useful and can be harnessed to create these new fantasy scenes in new ways.

This book shows you many of these basic diorama making techniques and will help you to create some amazing dioramas that will take your imagination to new heights.

About this Book

This book is several things but first and foremost it is a step-by-step guide that will take you through the whole process of making wonderful dioramas of fantasy and medieval scenes. It is also a great reference and resource to showing you all the various techniques and materials that will help you make great looking dioramas. Above all else it is a creative resource that will help unleash and develop your creativity in fantasy diorama making.

Suggestions for using this book

It is recommended that you read the whole book to get a sense of all the various techniques and tools that are used in diorama making before you start building one. The reason for this is that it will give you ideas on what kinds of creative things you want to put into your dioramas. You will also get a good sense for how much work and how much cost is involved in the various techniques so you can plan your time and budget accordingly. This book is also meant to be read as you create your diorama. You can turn the page and progress along in the book as you progress in the building of your dioramas.

About the Author

Will Kalif has been making dioramas for decades and has made them in all sizes, shapes, and themes ranging from as large as eight feet in length to as small as one foot square. He has also done some very unique dioramas. You can see his work and get more diorama information and tutorials on his website at www.stormthecastle.com.

Section 1
Some basics before beginning

The Scale of Your Diorama

The first thing you need to think about when making a diorama is the scale of the objects that will be incorporated into it.

This picture shows some typical fantasy miniatures in the 28 mm scale. The ruler is six inches long.

If you are going to be using miniatures or pre-fabricated items like buildings, items, treasure chests, vehicles, creatures, or any other type of thing you have to get a sense of their size so you can plan the diorama in a way that will make sense and look real. In other words, the diorama has to be in scale with the objects on it. It won't look right if your humanoids are 1 inch tall and the trees are one half inch tall!

It is always a good idea to purchase some sample miniatures and have them on hand before you start building a diorama. This way you can get a real sense for the size and height of things. You don't necessarily have to have all of the miniatures you plan on using but they should all be made using the same scale.

Understanding Miniature Scale

There are a variety of different scales that are used in fantasy miniatures and these scales have varied and changed a bit over the years. But the general rule of thumb you can use is the translation to six feet. Generally the scale given in millimeters equals six feet in real life. So in some of the more common scales of 25, 28, 30, and 35 mm each of these would represent six feet in real life. So an average human character would be about six feet and in the 25mm scale the miniature would be 25mm tall.

There are ten most commonly accepted scales for miniatures and here are the eight most popular:

2mm scale – This is a very small scale and is often used for gaming in tight spaces or with large numbers of player pieces.

6.2mm scale – This is a standard size for large scale historical battles.

10mm – Popular scale and is equivalent to the N-Scale Railroad train which makes it a good option if you want to use many of the diorama making materials that are available in N-Scale.

15mm – Very popular size for historical wargamers but not used in fantasy role playing games.

20mm – Very popular with WWII Wargamers and is equivalent to the HO Model Railroad scale which gives a lot of options for purchasing diorama materials made for railroad models.

25/28mm – This is the most popular size for fantasy gamers and is equivalent to the OO Scale in railroading. It's my favorite scale for dioramas and there is lots of railroad diorama making supplies that fit this scale. This book uses this scale in the tutorials.

30mm – Older scale and not used very much in modern times. It is a good match for S Scale model railroads.

54 mm – This scale is generally used for collectible figures; and miniatures in this size are often very detailed and well crafted. This size of miniature is often used in dioramas that specifically showcase one or just a few items. The goal of a diorama with this scale is more to highlight a specific piece or two rather than to build a complete landscape. This scale is a very close match to models in the 1:35 scale.

Translating millimeters to inches

One inch = 25.4 millimeters so it is easy to get a sense for how large a humanoid figure would be in these various scales. In the 25/28mm scale a human would be about 1 inch tall which equals 6 feet in size. In the 54mm scale a humanoid would be a little over two inches tall which equals 6 feet in size.

A couple of important things to think about when considering scale:

When making a diorama you should always stay within the same scale for that diorama. This will insure it looks real. If you were to use humanoids in the 25/28mm scale and then use horse in the 10mm scale they wouldn't look right. The horse would be about the size of a big dog. So no matter which scale you use just stay within it.

Scales effect on size, detail and cost of your diorama

The scale you use for your diorama will have an impact on the size of your diorama, the cost of it and the level of detail you can achieve. And to illustrate this let's consider a simple scene of a hunter standing next to his stone house. Let's picture a hunter in real life. He is standing outside the stone house he built. It is a single room stone building with a fireplace, bunk, table etc. In our minds eye we picture this house being about eighteen feet wide by eighteen feet deep and about twelve feet in height.

In the 25/28mm scale where 1 inch equals six feet the hut, when built for your diorama, would be about 3 inches wide, 3 inches deep and about two inches tall. This would make it look realistic and in scale to your Hunter miniature.

If you used a miniature in the 54mm scale the hut would be about 6.3 inches wide, 6.3 inches deep and about 4 inches tall.

With the larger scale the diorama would be twice as large which is an important consideration and it will probably be more expensive. But you will be able to make it with significantly more detail – it will look much more realistic. So this is the tradeoff you have to consider when choosing a scale.

I find the 25/28mm scale to be the best for my goals. It gives enough detail to be realistic, there are lots of miniatures available, and it is small enough so that I can make large dioramas that have a lot of detail and cover a lot of terrain.

A paper mock-up of a hunter and his stone hut

Create Mock-ups to help you see the scale

A very simple technique that I use before I start building a diorama is to create some quick and easy mock-ups using paper or cardboard. I make some of the major structures so I can place them with the miniatures and see if they look right.

The picture shown here uses the example of the hunter and his stone shack. By doing this you can get a quick feel for the scale of things in your future diorama and you also have a great way to arrange the different components of your diorama.

Graph paper is also a very handy tool to use at this stage of diorama making. It allows you to easily get a measurement on the size, scale, and relationship of objects in your diorama. This will come in handy later in the process when you start making the real diorama.

The Theme of Your Diorama

A diorama has one very basic and very important concept that you have to understand before you start building it. It is a frozen moment in time. Your diorama will display one very specific instant of time and this leads to a lot of creative variations that you can choose from or create.

The two components of your diorama

Your diorama will have two very distinct components: The figures and the scene.

Each of these components compliments the other to make up the overall diorama. You can design your diorama with either component first in mind and either way is right. For example you can get some miniatures and then develop a scene around them. Or you can decide you want a particular scene and then choose miniatures that will be right for the scene.

What will your miniatures be doing?

This moment in time can be the moment just before conflict (which will create a nice feeling of anticipation that something big is about to happen). Or it can be a moment in the middle of conflict (as in the battle between two combatants, or many combatants). It can be a scene showing the miniature figures doing whatever it is they do –dwarves can be mining, elves can be hunting, soldiers can be marching; or it can also be simply a scene that looks good and shows off your miniatures.

The important thing here is to give some thought to what the figures in your diorama will be doing. What is natural for them? Once you have this question answered you can start to think about the scene they will be in.

"Our warrior women contemplate a swim."

Location, location, location

The scene of your diorama will be what makes it really something special. And it is what makes it a real fantasy diorama. You have a lot of choices when it comes to the scene and you are only limited by your imagination. Here are some examples to give you an idea for what you might want to do.

Outdoor scenes:

- Outside a castle
- Within the castle walls
- In a Forest
- Along a River or stream
- Around a campfire
- On a battleground
- Under water
- In the sky
- On the wall of a castle
- On a glacier
- In a Jungle or Rainforest
- In a Desert
- On a farm
- Climbing on the side of a mountain
- Near a lake or the Ocean

Indoor Scenes

- In the Kings Hall
- Treasure room
- A Dungeon
- Inside a stone hut
- In a cave
- A Dwarven Mine
- An underwater cave
- A Dragon's Lair
- A small village
- Inside a Pub or Inn
- In an Elven Tree house

One more key to a creative and interesting diorama

Something that is often overlooked in diorama making is the full use of three dimensions. A diorama is not just a collection of objects on a flat surface – well, it can be, but it shouldn't be! Remember that you have all three dimensions to work in and to make it look really interesting. Think up and down. Put a cave underneath the surface of your diorama, or suspend objects in the sky above it. If you have mountains you can hollow them out and put levels right inside it. This consideration of the full three dimensions of space will make your diorama much more interesting to look at.

Section 2

Designing Your Diorama

Part 1: Begin on paper

Designing a diorama is much like designing a house or a public park. And just like an architect begins the design process on paper so you too should start your design work on a blank piece of paper. If you plan on making a large diorama (larger than a single sheet of paper) you should use graph paper. It will make it easy to measure and translate the design to a larger scale later when you are ready to build.

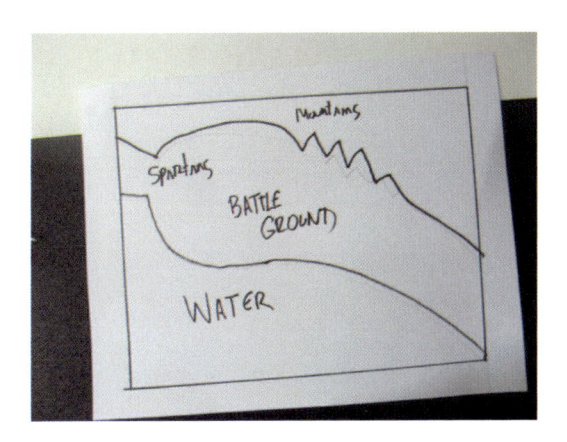

The Battle of Thermopylae design layout

This picture shows a drawing of a fantasy diorama called "The Battle of Thermopylae".

It will be a diorama that shows the battle between the Spartans and the Persians. On the left is the hot gate where the Spartans made their last stand. And on the right is the path that the Persians used to approach the battle.

The original plan is for this diorama to be maybe three feet in width. I used graph paper so I could translate the scale onto a larger paper.

This drawing is the end result of several dozen drawings and sketches.

It is very rare that you will actually just draw it out once and have a finished product. As you draw it you are going to want to make changes. Step back from it, take a look at it and keep working on it until you have a layout and design that you think is what you want. Be very free and loose with your drawings. Experiment with different ideas and different layouts. These experiments will often bring up some great ideas that will be very creative and look really good as a final design.

Remember that your diorama is three dimensional so make notes right on the paper as to where the high and low points are on the scene. Are there any specific terrain features such as rocks, cliffs, or water? Make a note of them right on the paper. If you are doing another level to your diorama like an underground cavern or a lower level of a building you should draw this out on a separate sheet of paper and coincide both drawings so if you placed one right on top of the other they would line up correctly –as they actually would in the diorama.

As the design of your diorama starts to take shape you can make small paper mock-ups and place them right on the design to get a good look at how things will be in three dimensions. It also allows you to move the various elements around.

The Important thing about designing on paper

The important thing to remember at this point of your diorama design is that nothing is yet set in stone! This is a process where you draw something out, take a look at it, change it, then draw it out some more. It is a slow working toward the eventual finished product. You don't just draw it out then build it. And the more time you spend in this part of the project the better your final product will be. Your eye will improve and you will get real good at this. All the work you do right now is well worth the effort and will save you a lot of time and energy later in the product.

The more you draw it the better it will get. This is the process that an artist uses when doing a drawing. If you keep working at it new possibilities open up and the drawing keeps getting better. It moves closer to what you envision it to be.

Part 2: Transferring the drawing to your diorama base

If you are doing a small diorama that is the same size you can easily translate the drawing on the paper right onto the board that will be your diorama base. You can just look at your drawing while you redraw the lines onto the wooden base or you can tape the drawing right onto the base then pressing down hard redraw the lines with a pencil or pen. When you remove the drawing you should be able to see the indented lines you drew right into the board. Just redraw them in pencil.

If you are doing a larger diorama (larger than a sheet of paper) you should get a large sheet of craft paper or a poster board and free hand draw the pattern onto the paper. Cut the paper or poster board to the intended size of your diorama before doing this.

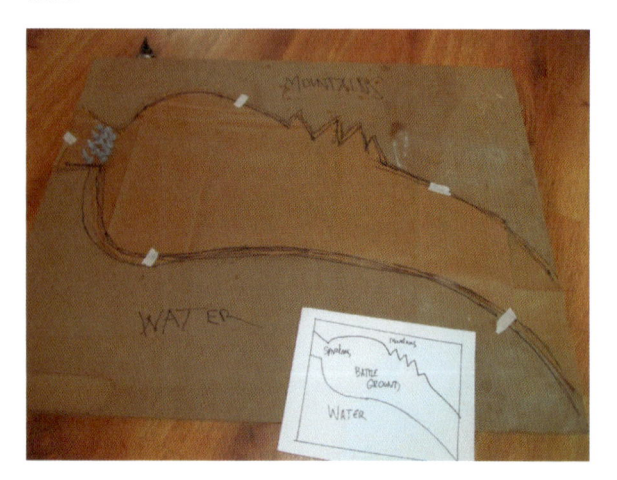

The small diorama drawing has been transferred to the large template.

In the above picture I have cut out a piece of packing paper to the completed size of my diorama (2 feet X 3 feet). I then freehand drew the pattern onto it. Gift wrapping paper works great for this. Just tape it down to a table surface so it doesn't curl up on you.

Notice how I have placed some miniatures right onto the large template. It's important to realize that you are still in the development stage of the diorama and things can still be changed. You may get to this size and realize you want to make some changes to how it looks, how things are laid out, or you may even want to change the size of the diorama itself. This is perfectly normal. You should go back and re-do your smaller sketches then re-do your large template. It is not uncommon to do this several times.

Easy tip for transferring the pattern

If you are having trouble accurately transferring the line drawings from your template to the base of the diorama you can cut it into pieces that follow the terrain then tape down the pieces and draw around them.

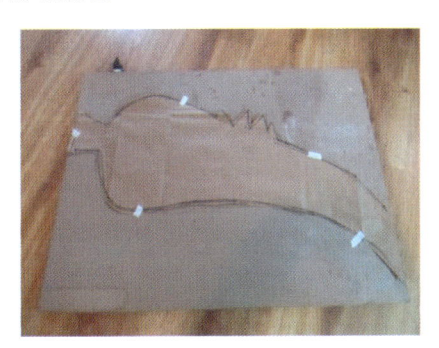

In the picture above I have cut out the template and taped it right down to the base of the diorama. Now I can draw lines right onto the base. Cut up your template in any way that makes sense and that makes it easy to transfer the lines.

Next you should finish the transfer of the design by filling in all the notes right onto the base. It is now ready for building.

Laying out the Medieval Village Diorama

Let's take a look at some of the layout for the medieval village. We will see a lot more of the medieval village diorama in this book.

The First diorama base we are looking at here is all about the terrain. But what if the diorama is all about buildings?

We could just draw squares and rectangles on the base to get a sense of the layout. But, remember that a diorama is three dimensional. It goes up too. And with something like a village we will want to take a look at how it will look in three dimensions.

The Medieval Village diorama will have a whole lot of buildings. So it is important for me to try to see how I am going to fit and arrange them. After I did my layouts and drawings on paper I made a series of cardstock buildings and put them on the wooden base that I made.

This is so I could arrange them, move them and see how they will all fit.

I just wanted to give you a sense of this. And if you are wondering about that white plaster skin we will be covering how to do that and a whole lot more in this book.

And while you are placing the buildings and the various large objects that will be part of the diorama you can also draw lines and notes on the wooden base. These lines and notes will help you in further steps.

The notes can help you understand things like rocky and rough terrain and how it will look. The following picture shows the medieval village diorama after the skin of plaster has been put on. See how it is rocky and mountainous on the far end to the left?

Section 3

Building Your Diorama

Part 1: The base of your diorama

If you are making a small diorama (less than two feet in any dimension) you can simply use a flat sheet of wood, plywood or MDF that is at least ½" thick. This will suffice.

(MDF is a building supply that comes in sheets. You can buy it at any home improvement store.)

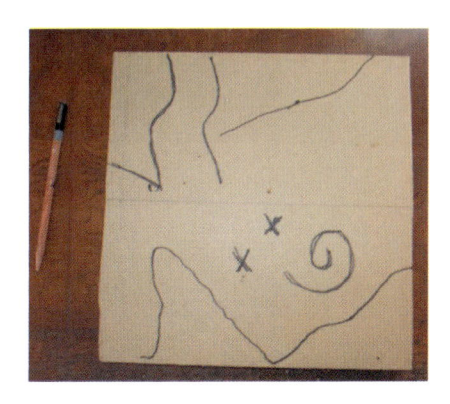

a small diorama base
(1/2" thick MDF or plywood)

Make sure it is not warped and that it can hold a couple of pounds of weight without bowing.

If you are making a larger diorama you should build some kind of a base. A larger diorama can weight twenty or thirty pounds once all the plaster and materials are placed on it. So you want it to be strong and you don't want it to warp.

A larger base (2' X 3')

The picture above shows the frame of a diorama that is two feet by three feet in size. I used two-by-threes and screwed them together. The surface of the diorama is the large sheet in the upper part of the picture. I nailed this sheet right down onto the base.

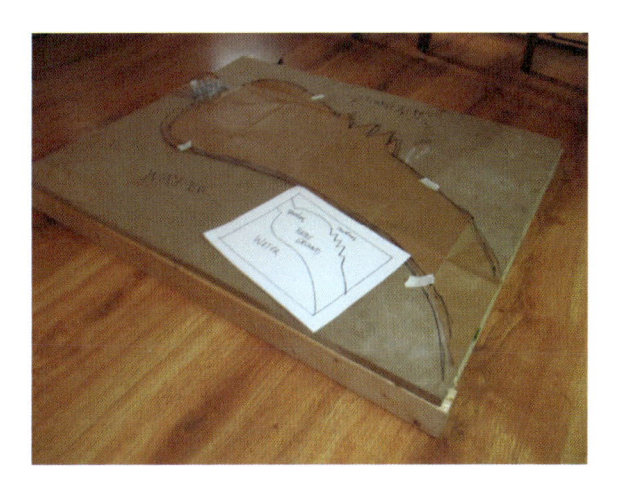

The surface is nailed onto the frame and the base is ready to go.

If you are building an unusually large diorama that is 5 feet long or more you may want to build a complete table for it. And it would be a good idea to put wheels on the bottom of the legs so you can roll it away from the wall to work on it.

This diorama is eight feet by four feet (one full sheet of plywood) and I built a complete table on wheels for it. I also used lag bolts to keep it all together nice and strong.

The general rule of thumb when making the base of your diorama is the bigger it is the stronger it has to be. And it is always okay to build it stronger than you think you need it. You don't want it to be frail when it is completed.

Unique and Unusual Shapes

Remember that a diorama is limited only by your imagination. This also means that the structure of the diorama can be unique too. It is not just the scene you are depicting but it is also the housing for it.

Just about anything you can imagine can be created for the diorama structure or base. A good example of this is the wall mounted diorama, which is often called a shadowbox.

In the pictures below I show you a wall diorama I made from an old window pane. I built the housing for the diorama and attached the window to it with hinges and a handle. This way it could easily be opened up to examine, clean or upgrade.

This wall diorama is thirty-five inches wide, twenty-nine inches tall and about five inches deep. The back of it is made of Luaun and the walls are simple two-by-fours.

(Luaun is a thin sheet of wood. You can buy it in any home improvement store)

The wall diorama shown in the picture above is part of this book.

In it I build an underground scene and I use foam. Foam is a great material for making dioramas. It is inexpensive, easy to work with and takes detail very well. I have a whole section on working with foam in this book.

Part 2: Building the terrain under structure

This is where you build the frame of the terrain. It gives the shape to the diorama. The basic concept is to build all of diorama from the ground up.

Needed Materials for this step:

- Masking Tape
- Strips of cereal box cardboard
- Strips of corrugated cardboard
- Plenty of newspaper
- Scissors

You use masking tape, newspaper and strips of cardboard to form the frame of the terrain.

This picture shows the frame almost complete.

This picture shows the completed diorama from a different angle. Notice the hill that the wizard is standing on.

The easiest and fastest way to do this is to simply use balls of newspaper and masking tape to build up the terrain.

And this method is okay for smaller dioramas. But if you are making a larger diorama you should use lots of cardboard strips to make a frame that is nice and strong and corrugated cardboard is the best.

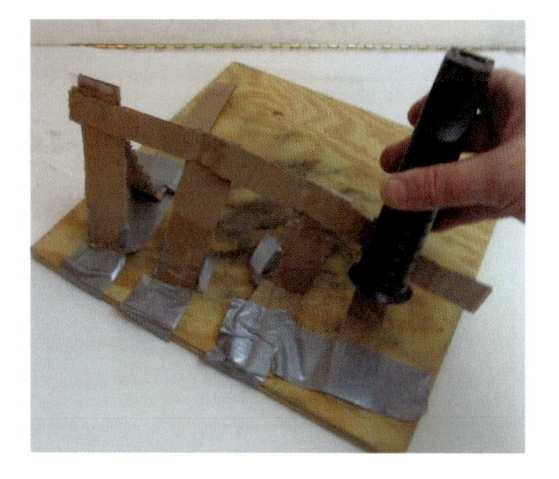

Larger dioramas need a stronger frame

In the picture directly above I am building a very large diorama and am creating a very strong frame using corrugated cardboard, tape, and even a stapler. When the frame is completed I will stuff it all with balls of newspaper.

The following picture shows the large diorama with a completed frame. It is stuffed with newspapers and ready for the surface of the terrain (the shell) to be applied.

The frame is complete and ready for next step

A Tip about Creating the Frame

The same rule applies to the frame as it did to when you were drawing out your diorama. Nothing is yet set in stone and you should experiment during this stage. Try different heights of terrain and see what looks right. Move your pieces of cardboard and balls of newspaper around. You can take pieces apart and try again. Keep working it until it looks the way you want it to.

Move the pieces around until they are right

In the previous picture you can see how there are lots of upright cardboard strips. This is the initial frame and it is just experimental. Move the pieces around and try different heights and shapes until you get it to look the way you want. The diorama in the picture is an extreme example of diorama making in that it has some sheer cliff walls. Most dioramas aren't this extreme but it is a good example of what can be done in this craft.

Here is a look at the medieval village terrain understructure

There are lots of strips of cardboard and it is stuffed nice and tight with wads of newspaper. But a good portion of the diorama is very flat. That is the area where most of the buildings will be sitting. I nailed down a sheet of cardboard in that spot.

Part 3: Doing some preparatory Wiring

If you are going to be adding special effects that require electricity this is a good time to run the wires -before you apply the plaster shell.

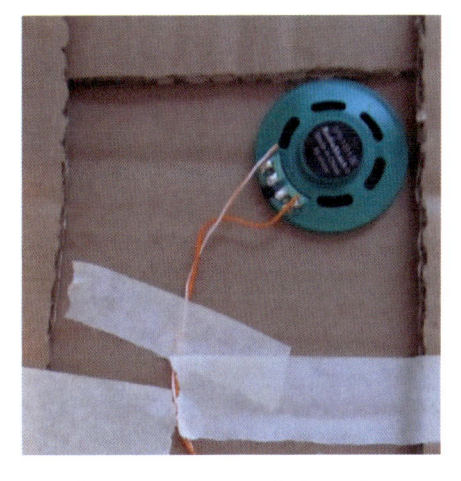

Speaker and wires added to diorama

This next picture shows the wires sticking up out of the surface of the medieval village. Each loop of wire is in the location of a building. You can see that each building will have electricity.

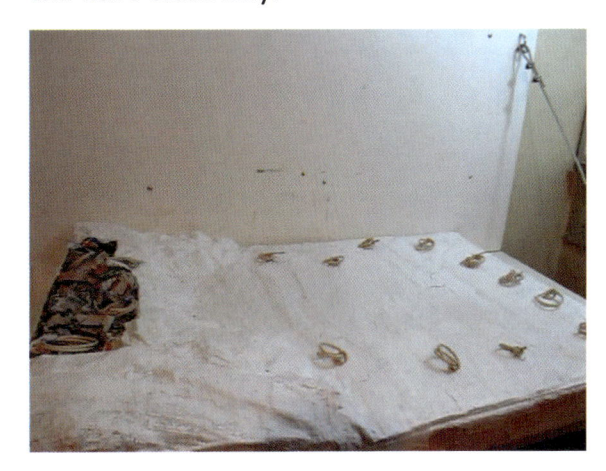

I will be covering more of how to wire up your diorama in a later part of this book. For now you should be thinking about this being the time to start some of the wiring. Once the plaster shell is completed you can still punch or drill holes in it and add wires.

It just is a bit more difficult.

In the next section we will learn how to apply plaster to the frame and make a smooth terrain.

Part 4: Applying the Terrain Shell

In this step of the process you apply sheets of either plaster cloth or paper towels to the terrain frame to make it a terrain shell. This shell will be the landscape of your diorama as shown in the next photo.

The Plaster shell has been applied to the diorama

There are four different methods you can use to create the terrain shell. The first three methods are traditional and long lasting. You can do professional work with these methods. The fourth method is cheap and easy but not as professional. You can still do good work with it but it is less sturdy and prone to getting a bit shabby over time. But, it is cheap and easy.

1. Plaster Cloth
2. Hydrocal with paper towel strips
3. Plaster of Paris with paper towel strips
4. Paper Mache (cheap and easy)

The basic concept involves laying plaster soaked strips of cloth or paper right down onto the frame of the diorama. When these strips harden they will form a shell that you can paint, or apply textures, trees, rocks or other terrain materials directly to. Think of it as the whole surface terrain of your diorama.

Method 1: Plaster Cloth

Plaster cloth is the easiest (and fastest) method for creating the terrain shell. It is sold in long strips that you cut and soak in water then simply lay right down onto the shell.

Using Plaster cloth

Plaster cloth is very similar to the material that is used when creating a cast on a broken arm or leg. Several different hobby companies make it and you can easily find it at any well-supplied craft or hobby shop or by doing an online search for "Plaster Cloth". Simply soak it in water for the recommended period then lay it onto the frame as shown in the photo below.

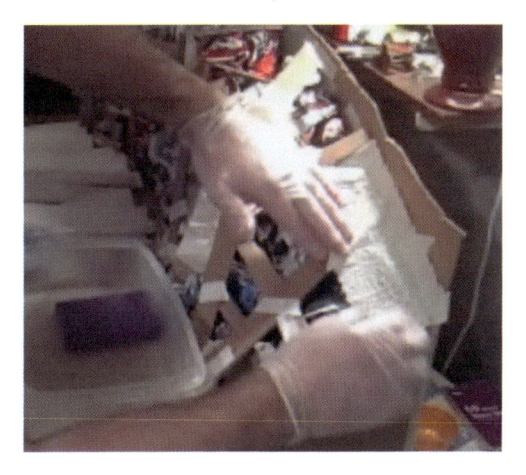

Plaster and Hydrocal can be an irritant to the skin, even cause burns. You should wear gloves as in the picture and always follow all safety instructions that come with the product.

Method 2: Hydrocal and paper towels

Hydrocal is a lightweight and strong material made specifically for dioramas and mold making. It is a type of plaster that dries very fast and is very workable. You can cut it, sculpt it, sand it, paint it, drill it, and work it in many different ways.

Hydrocal is the best way to make the diorama shell. It also makes the smoothest and best-looking shell. If you really want your diorama to come out the absolute best you should use Hydrocal.

It dries extremely quickly and you have to mix and use small batches. For a small diorama you may only need one batch but for a larger diorama you may need to mix up and use as many as ten batches.

Safety Note about Hydrocal: *Make sure you follow all the manufacturer's safety recommendations. It can burn the skin if allowed to harden so wear protective gear.*

How to do it

Before mixing your Hydrocal you should prepare yourself by cutting lots of strips of paper towels. Vary them in strips ranging from 1 to 3 inches in width. If possible, use the paper towels that have the reinforcing fibers in them. This will make the shell very strong and they are easier to work with when soaking them in the Hydrocal.

Quickly mix up a batch of Hydrocal according to the manufacturer's suggestion and soak a strip of paper towel in it. Use your fingers to wipe off the excess then lay it right down onto the terrain frame.

You need to work quickly because the mixture will dry in about five minutes so that is all the working time you have. When it becomes unworkable wash everything out of the bowl immediately and mix up a new batch. Continue making batches and applying the paper towels to your frame until it is complete.

A note about Hydrocal: Adding a bit more water to it makes it easier to work with but will not slow down the drying speed.

Method 3: Plaster of Paris

Plaster of Paris works almost as well as Hydrocal with the bonus that it is a little slower to dry so you have a bit more time to work with it. It is also more readily available. You follow the same procedure as you did with Hydrocal and mix a batch then soak paper towel strips in it.

Plaster of Paris also has some properties that can make it harmful.

It can generate a lot of heat which can burn unprotected skin so be sure to follow all of the manufacturer's safety suggestions.

When laying down the terrain shell you should always overlap the strips. This will make a strong shell. A general rule of thumb is to lay down a strip then cover one third to one half of it with the next strip. This will insure you have a strong shell, which can be support the weight of any terrain materials or structures you add to it.

Method 4: Paper Mache

Paper mache is good for terrain and landscaping as a base. But you have to remember that it is flour and water so unlike the previous three methods it is a foodstuff-like material and it is prone to moisture and even mold (over time).

Here is a picture of a diorama made with paper mache. It has stone like structures and mountain terrain area. It is Helms Deep from Lord of the Rings.

You do the same method as with the plasters by using strips of paper towel dipped in the paper mache mix.

Quick Paper Mache Recipe

You simply mix even amounts of plain white flour and water. Then add a tablespoon of salt. I typically mix two cups of flour and two cups of water then add the salt.

The salt is a mold prohibitor. It will give longevity to the diorama.

The picture below shows the initial stage of a paper mache diorama. You build the frame the same way you would for a plaster diorama. Make sure you make it nice and strong. And fill all the cavities with crumpled newspapers. The paper mache soaked paper can be very heavy and it can distort the shape of your diorama.

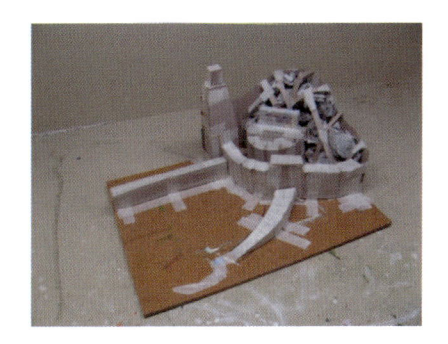

Cut up small strips of either newspaper or paper towels. Paper towels generally will give you better detail in your diorama.

Dip a strip in the mache mix, wipe off the excess and apply it to the diorama. Use the same technique as you would for plaster.

Overlap all the strips at least 1/3 on other strips and cover the whole diorama so it has at least two complete layers. When you are done you should set the diorama aside to dry for at least 24 hours before you begin the detail work.

As the diorama shell dries some of the paper towel or newspaper may curl and get distorted. You can easily touch this up and smooth things out with a wet sponge.

Part 5: Foam as an alternative for landscaping a diorama

There are several different ways to make the shell of your diorama and another effective way is to use foam or Styrofoam. This is a method that is used very effectively for war gaming and for large railroad terrain.

Foam is an excellent and easy product to use for making great dioramas. It is also relatively mess free. You don't have to worry about mixing and using plaster.

It can get a bit messy when you start cutting and carving it but this is easily remedied with a dustpan or vacuum.

And you can use it for just about every part of your diorama. The next picture is of a castle scene that I made totally out of foam. The whole diorama is foam (excluding the trees). The castle, castle walls, and the base are all made out of foam.

It does come in a lot of different types and in a lot of different sizes so you should know a little bit about it before you purchase or find any.

The next picture shows a selection of foams.

You can see that it comes in different colors, shapes, and sizes.

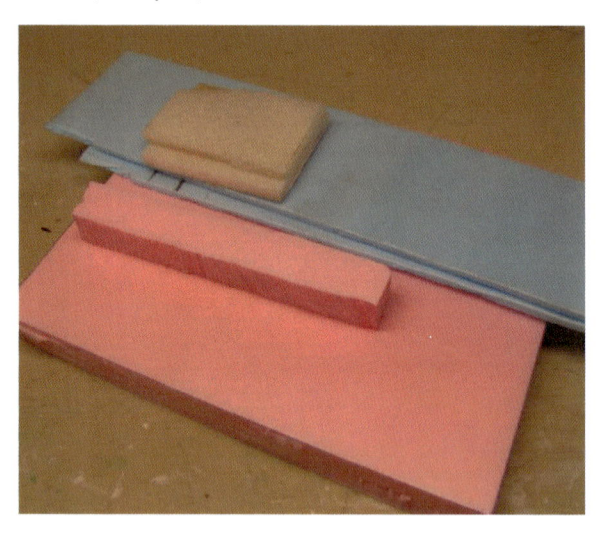

The pink product is called "Foamular" and it can be purchased in just about any home improvement store. It comes in large sheets as thick as two inches which makes it economical for dioramas.

The blue sheets are one half inch sheets of foam and the white pieces are foam specifically made for dioramas and terrain making. A company that makes a lot of great foam for terrain is Woodland Scenics and their products can be purchased at any hobby shop or online store.

Quality of foam

Most people are familiar with a product called "Styrofoam". This is very commonly used as a packaging product. You can often find it inside boxes of shipped products. But this type of foam is generally not optimal for terrain because it has a very rough consistency. It is usually made of small beads of foam that have been heated or pressed together. If you try to cut it you will have a difficult time getting accurate and clean details.

Before you start using a foam product for your terrain or diorama make sure you take a good look at it. The following two pictures show a good foam and a bad foam.

The following picture shows Styrofoam. It has a beaded appearance. While you can use it for dioramas you have to keep in mind that it will be difficult to accurately cut details into it. You can get pretty clean cuts if you use a wire cutter.

I will explain more about hot wire cutting after this.

The picture below is of foamular. This has a more uniform texture and it will take cutting and hot wire cutting much easier, and maintain much more detail. See how you don't see the little foam balls? The foam is much more fine grained.

But You can use the granular foam to your advantage in some circumstances

The pebbly effect can make some terrific ruins and textured walls and floors. Imagine a ruins. The pebbles are great for this. It's just a matter of painting it.

Tools and Methods for working with foam

You can work with a variety of tools when it comes to sculpting the foam. The most effective way to do lots of work quickly is to use some kind of a foam cutter. These foam cutters are called "Hot Wire" cutters because they use electricity to heat up a length of wire. The heat of the wire will allow it to melt right through the foam.

The picture above shows two standard hot wire cutters. The one on the left is a fork style where the hot wire goes across the two prongs of the "U". The cutter in the center is a wand style or knife cutter. The metal rod heats up and you use this to cut the foam.

These tools are inexpensive and well worth the investment if you are going to do a lot of foam work. I use the one on the left to make straight cuts in foam or to sculpt large areas. The wand style knife cutter is used for melting holes and for doing more detailed work.

Caution about cutting foam:

Not all foams are made to be melted, some can give off toxic or noxious fumes. Check the manufacturer's instructions before melting and always do this in a well-ventilated area.

The picture below shows the Hot Knife cutter easily cutting through the foam.

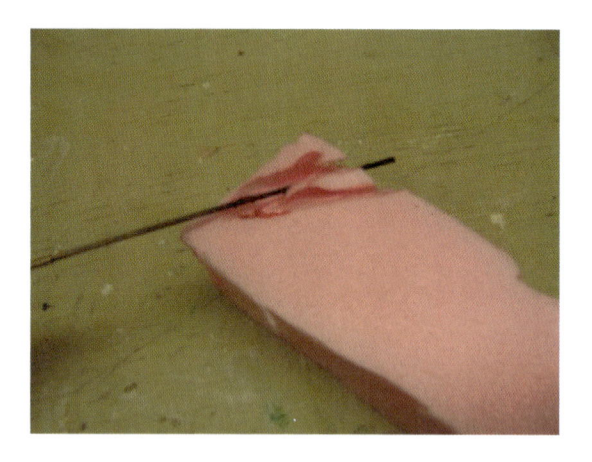

The following picture shows me using the hot wire knife to cut the crenellations in the top of the castle wall.

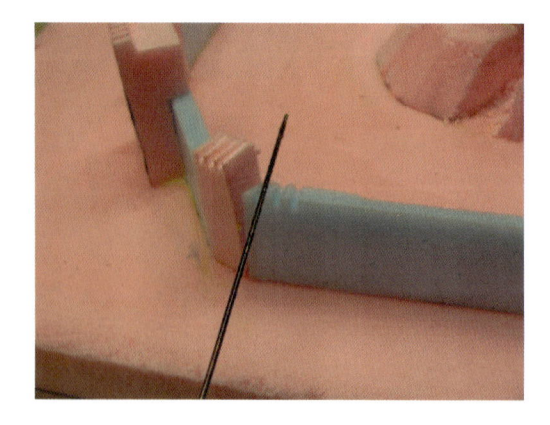

And the hot wire foam cutter is the best.

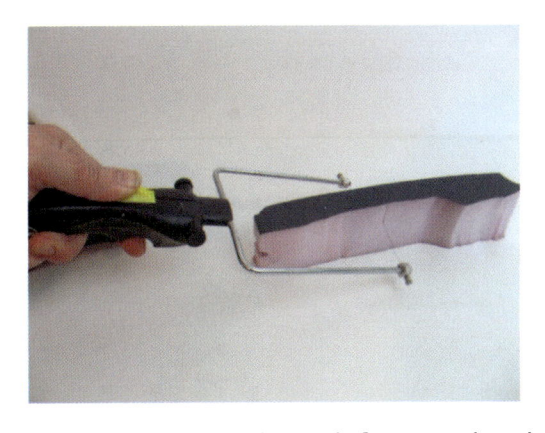

You can quickly cut through foam and make all kinds of shapes. If you are working with foam a lot it will be very useful to get one of these.

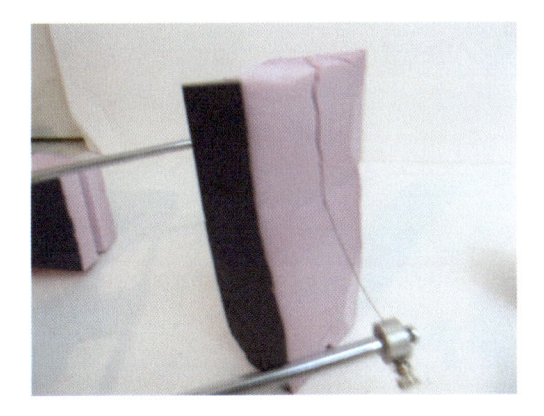

Using common tools other than heating tools

You can also use many other types of common tools such as x-acto knives, utility knives, files, sculpting cutting and carving tools. You can even use sandpaper to work on the foam.

The picture below shows the various sculpting and woodworking tools that I use to work with foam.

This ability to work with foam using a lot of different tools makes it very versatile and you can get a lot of detail with the right foam. The picture below shows the assembly of a castle keep. I used sandpaper to sand down squares of foam so they were cylindrical in shape and I used a hobby saw to cut them to size.

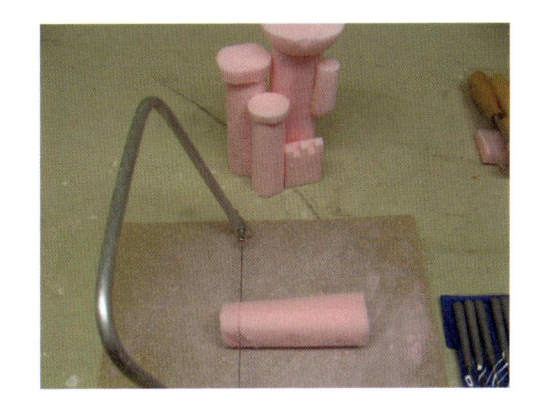

The Basic Assembly process for foam Dioramas

When laying out a diorama or war gaming terrain I recommend that you first do some sketches of what you want to create. These sketches will be a big help when it comes to actually building the terrain. Below is one of the sketches that I made for the terrain diorama in this tutorial. The end product will look very much like this.

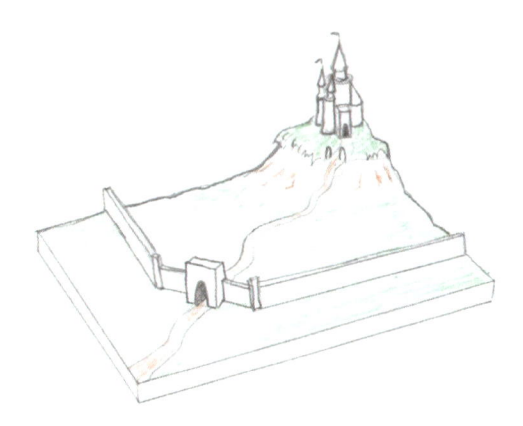

Select the types and sizes of foam that you will use and cut them to form the rough shapes of the terrain. I start with a single sheet as the ground. Then I add several different rough cut pieces to form the major landscape. In this example the major landscape is the hill/cliff that the castle is perched on. The picture also shows some of the castle walls. Generally I would not do this at this point of the game. But I may lay them out to see how they look. I wouldn't glue them in place until later.

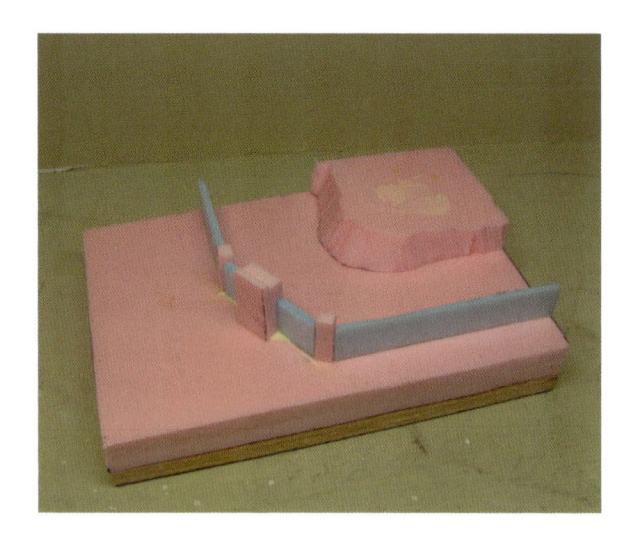

Next you glue the major parts in place. Remember that in this terrain I only have one high hill. In your terrain you may have lots of terrain features and you may have to glue various pieces. You can also layer the pieces so they are three, four or more pieces high. Use regular white glue, yellow glue or a glue gun to do this. Do not start sculpting the terrain until the glue is dry.

Ok, once you have all the major foam features laid out on the project you can begin with the detail and finishing work. The picture below shows all the major pieces in place.

The important thing to think about when doing the detail work is that you work your way down to the details. Start with the large and rough work such as cliffs and hills so you get the major shapes right. Then you work your way down to the finer details. The next picture shows me using a wire foam cutter to rough out the major shapes of the landscape.

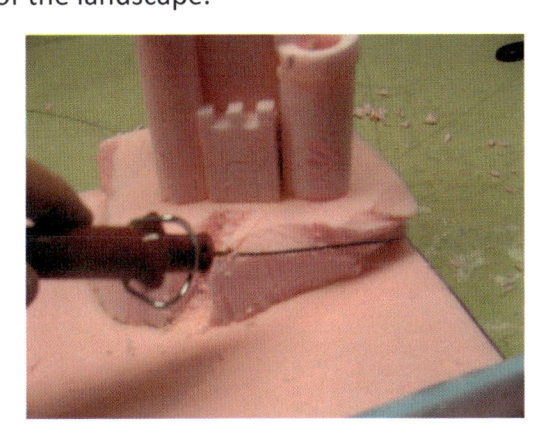

Once all the major landscape features are complete I begin doing the larger detail figures. I cut out a slot for the stairs then I sculpted the stairs from a piece of foam and glued it into place.

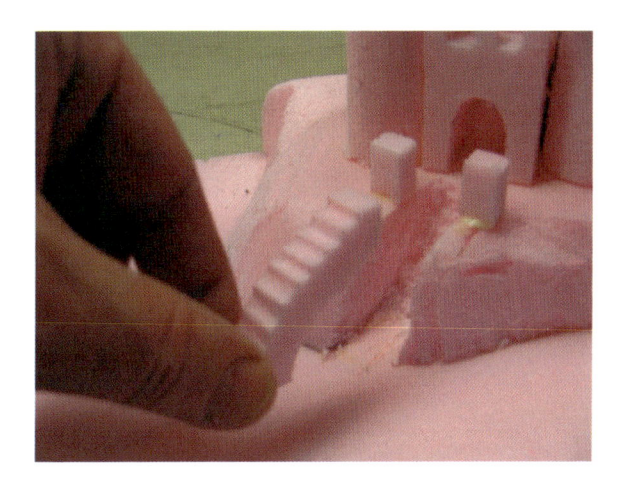

Foam terrain is flexible in this way. You can remove pieces, sculpt and cut away piece and sculpt pieces and add them in. Be creative.

One of the best things you can do is to use sheets of sandpaper to sand down the surface (ground) of the terrain.

 This will give it a landscape like look with peaks and valleys. The extreme flatness of the foam is not very appealing and doesn't look natural so sand it down a bit to give it some curves, peaks, and valleys.

Once all the sculpting details are done you are ready to do the typical landscaping painting and detail adding.

NOTE ABOUT PAINTING FOAM:

Foam and Foamular can be a bit sensitive when it comes to paint. Some paints will eat right through the foam. Spray paints are notorious for this. So, when making a diorama with foam always do some test painting in a small spot to check if the foam takes it ok.

Part 6: Painting the Terrain Shell

Whether you made your diorama out of cardboard and plaster or out of foam the following techniques still apply.

Now we are starting to move out of the craft part of making a diorama and moving into the arts part. If you are not an artist that is quite all right. There are some basic rules of thumb that will help you get this part right.

There are two different steps to painting your diorama.

1. The first step is simply painting raw colors over the whole diorama
2. The second part entails applying some detail colors

Beginning to build your terrain with a base coat of paint

The first thing you need to do is paint base colors onto your diorama. This part is quite easy. All you have to do is look at your design on paper and make some notes as to what kind of terrain is in what sections of the diorama. To understand how to do this let's take a look at a diorama.

A diorama of a wizard and skeletons

This is our simple wizard and skeleton diorama. It is one foot square and even though it is small it shows a lot of the basic traits of painting a diorama. There is water, grass, trees, rocks and dirt. These are the major components in most dioramas and they are all right here in this diorama. When you are painting the first coat of paint onto your diorama shell all you have to do is capture all these basic colors on the base.

Let's look at an overhead view of this diorama to get a better look.

Top view of the wizard diorama

Look at your diorama shell and look at your dra wings. What area has water? What area is dirt? What area is grassy? And what area is stone? Now all you have to do is paint a base coat right on the shell in these basic colors.

The color pattern for painting the shell

That picture shows an overlay of colors right on the shell of the diorama. I have broken down the diorama into its different major colors. You just paint these basic colors right onto the shell. And this is your base coat. When doing this patchwork base painting you don't apply the paint real thick.

It's not like you are painting a wall of your house. You just have to cover all of the plastered areas with a color. You can add water to the paint before you apply it so that it is dull and not too thick. This color is just a base that hides the plaster and covers any missing areas of texture that you will apply later.

A Little Bit about Paints and Colors

Getting natural colored paints can be a bit of a challenge if you never used paints before. The best paints for this are Earth Colors from a company called Woodland Scenics®. I use these colors almost exclusively but will occasionally use paints and colors from other manufacturers. These Earth Colors are specially formulated and really look fantastic. Well-stocked hobby shops will have them and other suitable paints. They are also very readily online at just about any hobby dealer or even large online stores.

This table gives you some rules of thumb for choosing colors based on what type of terrain.

Type of Terrain	Suitable Color
Grass	Green Undercoat
Sand/Desert	Yellow Ochre
Reddish Desert or Rust	Burnt Umber
Rocks/Cliffs	Stone Gray/Slate Gray
Dirt/Ground	Earth Undercoat
Water	Any Shade of Blue
Forest or Soil	Earth Undercoat
Stone or Concrete	Concrete

The Primary Colors of White and Black are very useful when used to either lighten or darken any of the above pigment colors. For example: When painting water you use solid navy blue for the deeper water then add some white to it to get a lighter shade as it moves closer to the shore.

This technique is very effective and very useful with all the terrain colors listed here.

Some Painting Tips for the first coat

- **Water:** (Shown as "A" in photo) In real life it looks very different near shore than it does away from shore. Generally, if you are using blue as a base you should use darker blue out away from shore and a lighter blue near the shore. You can easily achieve this affect by painting the darker blue area first then adding a little white to your paint and then painting the areas near shore. It will give you a nice uniform change from dark blue to light blue.
- **Is water always blue?** Remember that you might have a swampy area of your diorama or a brackish water section. Different shades of brown work well here.
- **Blending the colored patches** (This is shown in the photo as "B") One of the best things you can do is to blend the different patches of color where they meet. You don't want sharp lines that divide the green of grass from the brown of dirt. This doesn't happen in real life and it won't look natural on your diorama. So while you are applying

these base colors blend them where they meet. Let the green blend with the brown and the grey. It will make a smoother transition between the different patches of terrain.
- **Working with different shades of the same color** – You should vary the shades of the colors. In the example diorama there are a lot of variations between the same colors. You can see how the grey color varies from very dark to very light. This is achieved by either watering down the paint or by adding white. The green sections at the top of the diorama (Shown as "C") give a really good look at three different shades of the same color. The lighter greens were made by adding a lot of water. This technique of adding a lot of water is called "washing".

The Next Painting Step: Doing *some* detail work

Highlighting and varying the terrain color

Now you need to vary the colors a bit so it doesn't look so much like a quilt and it looks more like natural terrain. Highlighting is the best way to do this. Let's take a stone grey section of the diorama as an example. Get yourself a small dabble of the same color grey on your palette then add some white to it so it is a little lighter. Now you can use this new tone of grey to paint just small jagged parts of the diorama rocks that stick up -just doing the high points. This simulates how things look different depending on how they jut out from the terrain.

Washing with Black

Washing is a great technique for making the terrain look realistic. What you do is mix some black paint with water. Make it nice and wet so it drips and is pretty thin. Then you just wash over parts of the rocky terrain. The watery black will run down and gather in the low points and crevices of the surface of the terrain. This will make them much darker and it will look terrific.

These same techniques of highlighting and washing work for all the different terrain colors from stone to grass and dirt. When doing the grassy or forest areas instead of using black use a dark green. And for dirt areas use a dark brown. The chart on the previous page will give you a good rule of thumb for what colors to use.

Don't worry about the fine details

This isn't a fine detail-oriented step of the process. You don't need to be too meticulous with the colors. You will be applying textures over the whole terrain and most of this color will be completely covered. Now let's move on to the next step where you make and apply the terrain materials.

This image shows some nice black washing and highlighting with black and green

Part 7: Making and applying terrain features

Once the paint has dried we are ready to start adding all of the various textured terrain features to the diorama. This may include grass, dirt, trees, bushes, brush and other things.

Applying the textures to your diorama is a process of working from the ground up. You start with the finest textures –these are the closest to the ground. Then you work yourself up through more coarse textures until you eventually do the tallest textures which are bushes and the trees.

The Base Textures

The base textures are the ground textures. These are fine materials that you apply directly to the surface of the diorama and they come in a lot of different colors and texture coarseness. This layer of texture is what covers all of the paint that you previously applied. And the colors of these textures should be the same as, or very similar to the colors you previously painted the surface with. So for brownish dirt colored area you should apply brownish dirt like texture. The same thing applies for grassy areas etc.

(Three different consistencies in texture)

The image above shows three different densities of texture for the ground cover. The one on the left is a very fine powder. You should apply this first to the diorama. The texture in the middle is coarser and this would be applied second. The texture on the right is even coarser and it should be applied last. That coarsest one is typically used as bushes and plants.

When you are finished with this ground cover portion of the diorama all of it should be covered with texture, unless you specifically want some areas uncovered. These uncovered areas might be water sections or cliff/rocky sections. The texture covering won't be perfect and this is why you painted the diorama in basic colors These colors will hide any imperfections in the terrain texture layer.

> Using common household white glue works well for this. It will dry clear and you should just mix it with equal portions of water.

A Couple of notes about the three textures

Woodland scenic makes several different coarseness levels for ground covering texture and all of them are perfectly suited for the task. You also can change the number of different textures you apply based on the level of realism or detail you want to achieve. It is perfectly okay to just do one coarseness level and be done. The diorama will just not be as detailed. And if you do just one coarseness level it should be with the finest material like the one on the left in the picture above.

How to apply the Base Textures

Mix a small batch of white glue (an ounce or two) with an equal amount of water. Now apply this glue mixture to the shell of your diorama. Either spray it right onto the shell or brush it on with a paintbrush. Apply it liberally so the shell is nice and wet.

If you have a large diorama you want to do this in small patches no bigger than 8-10 inches square so it doesn't dry before you apply the terrain texture.

Woodland Scenics makes a perfect product for this called Scenic Cement. You can buy it in spray bottles or bottles without spray as a refill.

Now you can shake a thin layer of texture directly onto the glued area. And there are several handy ways to do this:

- You can put the texture material into a shaker much like a spice shaker and then shake it gently only to diorama. This is the best method.
- You can also fold a sheet of paper in half and pour some texture right into the fold then shake the paper gently over the diorama.
- You can also put texture on a sheet of paper and gently blow on it. And this technique works particularly well when you are trying to get texture onto vertical surfaces of your diorama.
- Experiment with texture applying techniques. Find the ways that work best for you. The important thing is that you apply a thin even coat on the surface.

Continue applying glue to the surface in small patches and continue applying the first layer of texture until all areas are covered in a base texture.

If you are going to do more than one coarseness layer it is recommended you allow the first layer to completely dry before you start a second layer. And when applying the second layer you should use a spray bottle to distribute the new layer of glue. Using a paintbrush on terrain already applied tends to bring it up or move it around which could cause unsightly patches.

Spice shakers make perfect containers for shaking terrain textures onto your diorama.

Using a folded sheet of paper also works well for sprinkling textures neatly and accurately.

Adding talus, stones, small pebbles or ballast material

Once you have the base layer of texture in place you may want to add talus or other small pebble like textures. You can do this with the same method of spraying glue then sprinkling on the talus. If you have trouble getting this coarser texture to stick you can mix it with the glue in a small bowl or cup then pour it directly onto the diorama. Don't make it too liquid though. It may cause your diorama shell to get soggy and sag.

Applying the Coarse Details to the Diorama

Before you start applying the coarse materials and terrain features to the diorama you should clean it and inspect it.

Once you are sure all of the glue is dried you should remove any excess terrain material by gently tipping the diorama to allow free material to fall off. If you have a large diorama and it is impractical to tilt it you can use a vacuum cleaner to vacuum off any loose material.

This step is necessary so you can see if there are any sections you did that do not have a good look to them or sections that the material did not adhere to. You don't want to fix these areas after you have applied more terrain materials. Just go back and re-apply glue and terrain texture to them which fills any open spots.

Once this is done you can then move on to the rough terrain features like bushes, grass stalks and trees.

Rough Terrain Features Like bushes, grass stalks and trees

This is where your diorama takes on a realistic look and this is where diorama making really goes from being a craft to being an art. You have to visualize how natural terrain looks and try to duplicate it.

Tip: Seeing things as an artist does

If you want to get really good looking terrain you need to look at terrain! Whenever you are outside you should notice how terrain looks. Notice how it clings in different areas. On the side of a cliff you can notice how small plants will grow out of cracks. Or notice how moss grows along one side of a tree. It is these little details that will make a big difference. You can do lots of research on the internet. The important thing about this is that if you want your diorama to look realistic you have to look at real things then mimic them.

With Rough Terrain less can be more

The picture above shows a nice use of rougher terrain. This is the rule when it comes to rougher terrain – use less of it. And try to place it in ways that look natural. Generally the bigger the terrain material the less of it you will use.

The above picture shows another good application of rough terrain materials. The bushes are clinging to the edge of the cliff just as they might in real life.

You can apply these rough textures to the surface of the diorama by putting full strength white glue on them and then sticking them directly to the shell. You should then spray over it with your watered solution of glue. This will insure that the various clumps of rough texture don't fall apart. The bush will stay intact once the sprayed on glue dries.

Terrain Tip

To get the upright stalks of grass you can purchase materials from woodland scenics or you can make them from old paintbrushes. Simply cut the bristles off the paintbrush then glue them in upright clumps directly to the surface of the diorama. Put a bead of white glue directly on the diorama and give it a few minutes to get stiff then stand the bristles right up in it. Hold them in place for a minute until they can stand on their own.

Bristles of a paintbrush. Now just stick the flat end right down onto the dab of glue on the diorama.

Tall Grass with Electro-Static Flocking

You can get really tall grass in your diorama and it really stands up tall. You do this with a tool called an electro-static flocker.

The electro-static flocker is a handy little tool.

The picture above shows it in action. There is a little bowl with a screen in it. You put the terrain grass in there and shake above the terrain.

There is a charge on the grass as it passes through the screen. You can see in the picture that there is a pin and a clip on the surface of the terrain. That applies the other polarity of charge. This causes the strands of grass to be repelled and they stand on end. Pretty neat and ingenious little device.

It does take a little bit of practice and to work well you hold the screened cup close to the terrain.

Section 4

Trees, Water, and Rocks

Trees

Trees come in a very wide variety of sizes and styles that mimic real trees. And they come with a lot of different foliage in a variety of colors.

If you have a specific theme you are trying to achieve or a specific location you will need to get the appropriate trees. Conifer trees which are pines and firs look quite a bit different than Deciduous trees which are the types of trees that lose their leaves in winter. And of course this is critical if you are doing a winter scene.

One of the most important aspects of tree selection is choosing trees that are of an appropriate scale. You should try a variety of sample trees so you can see what lends the right look to your diorama. Place them next to your miniatures (if you are using miniatures) to get a sense of the scale and if the tree size will look right.

The center tree in the above picture shows the attached base. You glue the tree into this base which makes it easy for the tree to stand up in the diorama. Typically you would apply terrain textures to the base so it blends in with the surface of the diorama.

Optional (preferred) Method of Tree Insertion

As an alternative to using the plastic tree base you can pierce a hole in the diorama landscape and glue the tree right into it. This is the method that I use because it looks more realistic.

Step 1 to inserting a tree: Punch a hole in your diorama

Step 2: Put some white glue in the hole, give it a minute or two to get tacky then insert the tree into the hole and hold it in place.

The Tree looks great!

Adding Foliage to the trees

To get a really good look to your trees you should add foliage with a variety of colors. Typically two or three different shades of green look realistic. You should also consider the type of tree and the season of your diorama. Woodland Scenics makes a lot of different foliage colors.

How to Add the Foliage to the trees

The plastic that the tree armatures is made of is very pliable and when shipped it is flat. You should gently bend it into a three dimensional (tree-like) shape.

Then apply a high tack glue to it. Woodland Scenics makes a glue called Hob-e-Tac that is specially designed for this. You apply it liberally to the tree armature and then set it aside for about 15 minutes so it sets into a very sticky form. You can use alternative glues. Just look for very high tack glue and let it set until it gets very tacky. This can be a bit frustrating and you have to be patient. When you dip the tree in the foliage bag it should stick very nicely. If it doesn't stick easily and tightly you either should use another type of glue or wait longer for it to get tackier.

Apply the glue to the tree then let it sit until it gets very tacky. For hob-e-tac this is about 15 minutes.

Once the glue is nice and tacky dip it in a bag of foliage. You may want to prepare the foliage first by breaking up large clumps.

Dip the tree in the bag of foliage and move it around so lots of foliage is applied.

And do this process with several different foliage colors. If you tree is green you should use several different shades of green.

Between applications of foliage use more glue and visually inspect the tree and make small adjustments to the placement of foliage.

Additional note about the tree armatures

You can cut the trees to any size you want and if you are looking for smaller trees or bushes you can even use just branches that you cut off of the main armature.

Trees aren't always full of foliage. Sometimes you can get a real attractive look by just putting a small amount of foliage on them. This gives them a sparse and almost dead look. This works great if your trees will be placed in terrain that is dead, desert-like or poor in plant life.

This tree shown in the next picture is a good example of a creative use of a tree armature and its foliage. It is clinging to the side of a cliff and has that typical look of bare-branches with just a small tuft of foliage at the end.

A Note about improvising trees and bushes:

Can you use real branches from outside trees? The quick answer to this is no! While they may look great they don't have a good life span. They will rot and turn colors. They will not stay preserved for a long period of time. When using artificial trees you are guaranteed they will stay exactly how you made them for many years.

Improvising and making your own tree armatures

You can make acceptable tree armatures out of wire. It takes a little practice but they will come out quite good.

To do it you will need two pair of pliers, some wire cutters and some wire. I use 14 gauge house wire but any kind of wire from an appliance or extension cord will also work well.

Strip out pieces of wire and then using the pliers you twist them into a tree shape. One end is all twisted together to form the trunk and on the other end all of the branches are separate. Move the wires that are branches so they stick out in a variety of positions like the branches of a tree.

Next you paint the trunk of the wire tree a brown color and set it aside to dry. Once dry you apply a liberal amount of a high tack glue to all parts of the branches. It goes everywhere except on the trunk. Then you set it aside to let the glue get very tacky. If you are using Hob-e-tac the recommended wait time is fifteen minutes.

Once you have waited the required period of time you dip the tree in a bag of foliage and move it around so all the branches are covered.

Set it aside to dry and once dry you can touch it up by adding a little more glue and a little more foliage.

The process of making trees takes a little bit of practice but you will get good at it. And using wire is a little bit of a challenge but your trees will come out great.

Tree Tips:

Trees aren't a uniform color. You should do every tree with at least two different shades of green. This is how they look in real life and it will lend maximum realism to your miniature trees.

They come in different shapes and sizes and with differing amounts of foliage. Remember to make them all unique.

Just about any type of wire can be used, even stranded wire. And stranded wire is easier to work with.

Getting your wire trees to look more realistic

You can use various modeling epoxies to get your trees to look even more realistic. You apply the epoxy or clay to the trunk and carve it into the desired shape and look. There are several inexpensive clays you can use to do this with. Super Sculpey® is an easy to work with clay that is baked in an oven to harden.

There are also several different types of two-part epoxies that you can use including ProCreate®, Green Stuff® or Kneadatite®. The two part epoxies are composed of two different segments that you knead together and over a period of time they harden.

If you want very realistic looking trees this is a great way to do it. But generally you cannot do the branches of the trees because the sculpting material will not hold properly. You just paint these wires brown and then cover them with the tree foliage.

Water and water effects

Adding water to your diorama is one of the best ways to make it look very real. Bodies of water and water effects can transform an average diorama into something special.

There are several techniques you can use for adding water and I will go over them.

Using Woodland Scenics Realistic Water©

Woodland Scenics makes a product called Realistic Water. It is a liquid that comes in a bottle. You simply pour a thin layer into your diorama then let it air dry. Once it has dried you can pour another thin layer and continue this until the desired thick is achieved. This is the easiest way to make water but it can be a bit costly if you have large water areas.

How to do it

The preparation work is important when you are adding water to your diorama. You have to make sure all of the water area is sealed with some kind of paint and you have to make sure the area to be filled is properly shaped. Water flows downhill and when you pour the realistic water it will flow downhill so make sure your water area is shaped correctly.

Here are the steps:

- Make sure the area for water is shaped in a way that it contains all the liquid. If your water area is on the edge of your diorama then add some kind of a border to hold the water in while it dries. This border you build will be permanent because the Realistic Water will stick to it like glue and harden.

- Make sure all parts of the diorama shell are painted. This will seal it. If the Realistic Water comes in direct contact with an unpainted plaster shell section it can soak through and leak or make the shell sag. So paint it and give it a second coat.

- Put terrain textures and extra items on the bottom before you begin pouring the water. This could include sunken items, pebbles, small shells, rocks, or anything you want to see through the water.

The picture above shows a corner of a small diorama that is ready for the water. The water area forms a nice depression, it is well painted, and I have built up a cardboard wall around the edges. Good to go and ready for the water to be poured.

Slowly pour the Realistic Water into the cavity allowing it to flow into all of the area you want covered. And make it no more than 1/8 of an inch thick. Use a toothpick to gently move it around so it flows into all the area to be covered. You want it to be a thin and even coat.

Allow it to dry for 24 hours before adding another layer and do not do more than three layers. You can get it to dry faster by using a fan but do not use heat or a hair dryer.

Adding Details and textures to your water

Rippled effects – You can get your water to have permanent ripples and other surface effects by waiting until it is almost hardened. Then you can brush it using a regular small paint brush or other types of tools even a toothpick or the handle of a spoon. Or you can place objects on the surface and they will adhere when it dries.

Paying attention to the shoreline

The shoreline is very important in a water scene. You should spend time working on the details around the shore of the water. Add small pebbles and marshy type bushes to make it look good.

The picture above shows our waterline on a similar diorama. Notice the variety of things along the shore. There are small pebbles, small clumps of foliage and some tall reed like plants.

Changing the Colors of your water

Realistic Water is water soluble so before you pour it you can add different colors or dyes to it to get a particular look. Some suggested colors are blue, brown or green. This all depends on the look you are trying to achieve.

Alternatives to Using Realistic Water

If you want to get deeper water you cannot use Realistic water. It is recommended for thicknesses of up to 3/8 inch. To go thicker you have a couple of other options.

Clear Casting resin – This is a product that

comes in a 32 ounce can. It is two parts and you mix the resin with drops of a catalyst and then pour it. Clear casting resin looks great and works great but it is a bit of a challenge. You have to mix it correctly and this depends on how much you are going to pour so you have to accurately judge how much you will pour. It also gives off toxic fumes so you absolutely have to use it and pour it and let it dry either outdoors or in a well-ventilated room. I recommend a room with a window fan set up.

While it is a bit of a challenge to use casting resin can create some really good looking water bodies and water effects.

Lexan (or Plexiglas) - Lexan is a plastic type of product that comes in sheets. Think of it as plastic sheets of glass but not as dangerous. You can cut it into any shape you want and use this as the surface of your water. In effect you can create a space between the bottom of your diorama and the surface of the water. In this space you can place under water objects.

Several ways to use Lexan as water

Lexan has several different ways that it can be used. You can paint the top surface of the lexan a water color and place it right into your diorama. If you paint it blue it will become the surface of the water and you won't see through it. This is the easiest method.

You can paint the bottom surface of the lexan, which is a bit more attractive. Now the water will have a little bit of depth and it will look more realistic.

You can get a more complex, and more attractive look if you create the underwater scene and bottom surface of the water with lots of details then place a clear sheet of lexan at the height of the water surface. This way you have the water and you can see through it to the bottom. And to make it even more realistic you can paint the top surface of the lexan with a clear lacquer or matte. This will give it a watery look.

Using lexan can be a challenge but it can also be very cost effective if you are making large bodies of water. You also have to prepare for this because the lexan has to be installed so you have to plan for this in the early stages of the diorama. You also have to take some time when making the banks around the water body. You have to be meticulous with terrain materials so they blend with the edges of the lexan in a natural way.

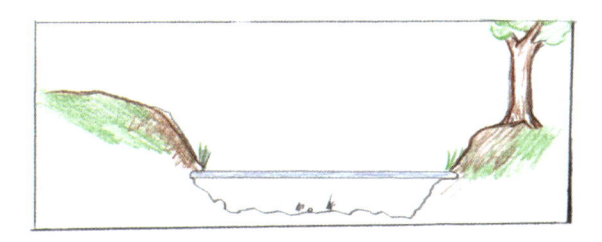

The above drawing shows lexan installed in the diorama. This lexan is clear so you can see the details at the bottom of the water body. And notice how the lexan is incorporated right into the terrain. This way you can create bank materials right on top of it at the edges to get a natural look.

Make a realistic Waterfall

The picture above shows a nice little diorama called "The secret grotto". It showcases a nice waterfall that looks real but is home made.

Here is the process for making the waterfall with just a few basic materials.

Some wax paper, a caulking gun and some DAP Crystal Clear Caulk.

That's pretty much it! You should have a little bit of white paint too so you can touch it up. And, I will show you some other options for getting the waterfall really professional looking.

You can get this caulk at any hardware store like Lowe's or Home Depot etc. It is very common. And DAP makes a few different types. Just as long as it is labeled "Crystal Clear" you will be good. I like this exact type because it has antimicrobial properties and it dries in 3 hours.

Cut a big square of wax paper and tape it down to a surface. Then apply strips of the caulk as shown in the picture. Be sure to measure the size waterfall you need and make the strips longer. You can trim them to size later.

Just lay out a series of caulk strips side by side and put them right up against each other so they will adhere together into a single piece.

Use a toothpick or some kind of a thin wooden implement to put lots of lines in the waterfall. Be sure to push together the various caulk strips so they are bound together as a single piece. Run lots of vertical creases so it looks like water flowing.

I recommend that while you have everything ready you make several of these even if you only need one. This way you can experiment with them and have some spares in case you cut it too short or something else happens. Won't hurt to make a few extra ones.

Now just let it dry.

Once it is dry you can peel it off the wax paper. It might be tricky and it is quite alright if some of the wax paper stays on the back. You wont be able to see it anyway.

This caulk is a bit flimsy and it won't hold up well on the diorama so we make a stronger backing for it.

Just cut a strip out of a 2 liter bottle. Make the strip about the width of your desired waterfall but make the lenght several inches longer. You will trim the length when ready to install it.

Bending the Plastic backing: Use a hair dryer on low setting to bend the plastic strip into the desired shape. Place it on your diorama, get a sense for where it should bend - then heat. Do this several times to get it to have just the bend you want.

Now glue the caulk waterfall to the plastic backing that you previously bent. You have a few different options when it comes to glueing. You can use a glue gun, or you can use a glue called "Cyanoacrylate" This works the best. But, you can try other glues and see how they work. You might have to experiment a bit with glue because some glues might not take to the caulk very well.

You can experiment with this and it was a great idea to lay out a few extra waterfalls with the caulk.

Trim the waterfall to the desired size and then glue it in place. You can use your DAP crystal clear or you can use the cyanocrylate or even a hot glue gun. As before you can experiment with various glues. But you want something that will dry clear.

Now you can accent it by painting small vertical bands of white on it. Use watered down white paint and apply it sparingly. You don't want to cover the waterfall. You just want to add accents as if there is foamy and frothy water.

You can use the caulk at both the top and bottom of the waterfall to get the textured bubbling and wavy effect. And once it is dry you can paint it.

Just apply some of the DAP and then sculpt it a bit with a brush.

Waves in Water

You can use a wide variety of products to make water effects like waves and ripples. You can use th DAP but there are other products that work very well for this kind of effect. Glazing mediums are an art product and they come in different consistences including medium and super heavy. You can brush these onto the water areas and then use a brush or other tool to make wave shapes and ripples.

This picture shows the use of a medium gloss gel to make waves. Notice how the tips of the waves are white. That won't stay. When it dries it will be clear. So, if you want the white caps you should add a little white pigment or paint it after it dries.

Here is a close-up of the waves using a heavy gloss gel.

Rocks, Stone and Cliffs

Adding rocks, stones and various types of cliff formations to your diorama can make quite a dramatic difference in how the diorama looks. There are a few different ways you can add these effects. First you can actually use rocks and stones that you find outside. Second you can purchase rubber molds that you can cast plaster into. Third you can make your own rubber molds. I will cover all three of these techniques in this chapter.

Part 1: Using Found Rocks and Stones

This is an inexpensive way to add some great formations to your diorama and all you have to do is search around for interesting rocks and stones. But a couple of things you have to be aware of.

- Make sure you wash the stones and rocks thoroughly. You don't want some kind of mold or fungus to contaminate your diorama.
- You have to consider the scale of your diorama. Keep this in mind when hunting for rocks. Generally you look for rocks and stones that have very fine details or are have lots of interesting sharp edges.
- You can use a hammer to break up the stones into more interesting and smaller shapes but if you do make sure you do it safely. Use only a

hammer approved for rock chipping and be sure to wear safety glasses.
- These found rocks do not have to remain exactly as you find them. You can paint them or add terrain textures to them to spice them up a bit.

Part 2: Purchasing Rubber Molds

Many hobby shops and train specialty shops will carry a large selection of rubber molds that come in great pre-made stone and cliff shapes. You can also purchase them in pre-made stone wall shapes.

The picture above shows several rubber rock molds. They come in a very wide variety of shapes and sizes.

How to cast rocks in Molds

Materials Needed:

1. A mold
2. A spray bottle
3. Water
4. Liquid Soap
5. Hydrocal or Plaster of Paris

What to do:

1. Put a few drops of liquid soap in the spray bottle then lightly spray the inside of the mold where you will pour the plaster or Hydrocal. The liquid soap will help prevent sticking and will help prevent bubbles from forming in your rock formation.
2. Mix up the Hydrocal or Plaster of Paris according to the manufacturer's directions and pour it slowly into the mold.
3. Gently tap the mold to release any air bubbles.
4. Let it dry
5. Once it is dry you can carefully remove the rocks from the mold by peeling the mold away or popping out the plaster.
6. Note, if the plaster rock cracks it will be ok. The crack will be perfectly aligned and the two parts can be glued back together easily.

How to make fantasy and medieval dioramas

The picture above shows several different shaped rocks that have been cast in rubber molds.

Part 3: Making Your Own Latex Rubber Molds

You can get a lot of variety in your stone shapes and you can even create stone walls by creating your own Latex Rubber molds. This is a very easy process and all you have to do is apply Latex Rubber in layers to the desired object.

Let's assume you are making a mold of a rock that you have found. The first thing you do is paint on a layer of Latex Rubber then let it dry for at least thirty minutes. Make sure you apply the Latex thoroughly so it gets inside all the crevices.

Step 1: Painting the latex on

Once this first layer is dry you proceed to paint on a second layer of rubber. Once that is dried you should do a third and fourth coat, always letting it dry between coats.

If you are only going to be making a few castings from this mold then three or four coats are sufficient. But if you want to use this mold over and over and keep it for many years then you should apply at least two or three more coats of rubber. And, after the third coat, while

Step 2: Separate the mold from the model

it is still wet you should cover it with cheesecloth. This will make it extra strong and durable. Then once this third coat, covered in the cheesecloth, dries you can go ahead and paint on the next few layers allowing time in between layers for drying. Using this layer of cheesecloth will give you a very strong rubber mold.

Step 3: pouring plaster into the latex mold

Latex rubber is inexpensive and easy to work with. This is a great way to add some real detail to your diorama.

Adding Rocks, Stone and Cliffs

Part 1: Painting and detailing the Rocks and Cliffs

Part of what you want to do when painting rocks and cliffs is to integrate the colors correctly into the landscape of your diorama. This will mean there will be a variety of different colors.

If, for example, your diorama is a desert scene the rocks and stone might be a shade of sandstone or some shade of red. This is important to consider when painting rocks and cliffs.

For this tutorial I am going to show you how to paint the rocks a standard slate gray color. This is a pretty typical color. The steps I take with this color are applicable with any color.

Note: You can use this painting technique on found stones too!

Step 1: Apply sparing amounts of your dark color to high points of the rock. In this example I use Stone Gray.

Step 2: While the paint is still wet apply a liberal coat of water. This technique is called washing and it washes the dark color all around the surface of the stone. The dark color will accumulate in the cracks of the stone giving it a very realistic look.

Step 3: Apply small amounts of white glue to various parts of the stone, brush it around a little bit with a paintbrush then sprinkle terrain texture on it. This gives the stone a dirty and realistic look.

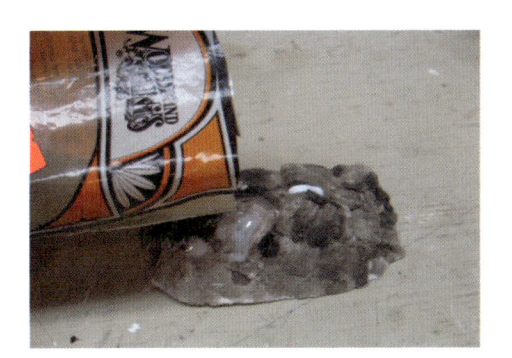

The picture below shows the terrain texture glued to the stone.

Step 4: Finish off the rock by applying large textures such as shrubs and grass bits.

Apply small spots of glue and some thin lines along the high lines of the stone.

And affix small bits of rough texture to the stone. The picture below shows the completed stone.

It is now ready to be placed in your diorama.

Part 2: Installing the rocks and cliffs

Affixing the stones to your diorama can be done in any of several ways. You can simply apply glue to the back of the stone and glue it right in place. Or you can cut out portions of the shell of your diorama to set the stone in place. Either way will be effective and you can use regular white glue to do this but if your stone doesn't sit well into the diorama, which can happen with larger stones you can use a Woodland Scenics product called Flex Paste. This is a flexible paste that will fill in the space behind the rock and give you a good attachment to the diorama shell.

Once you have affixed the stone to the diorama you will want to touch it up with small amounts of terrain texture to insure it looks natural. Simply apply small amounts of glue around any edges between the stone and the diorama and then sprinkle on terrain textures.

Alternatives to Plaster or Hydrocal: Cork and Real Stone

Real stone can be used on your diorama but you have to be careful when choosing the stones. It is often very effective to break up larger stones so they have a varied look that is more detailed. You can break stones with a hammer but be sure to wear safety glasses.

Using Cork in your diorama

Cork is an extremely effective alternative to casting stones. Typical wine corks can be broken up into a variety of interesting shapes and they can be painted to look exactly like stone. The use of cork is particularly effective if you want to create rubble in your scene.

You can break up the cork with a pair of pliers. Tearing it into a variety of shapes.

You can then place the cork pieces on your diorama to get a feel for how they look. The diorama pictured below is a simple rubble scene where some kind of a building has been destroyed. You can see the various pieces of cork in place.

Once you have gotten a good feel for how the cork is placed you can either remove it all and paint it or glue it in place and paint it in place. The picture below shows the painted cork pieces on the rubble diorama.

The Art of Improvising

An important thing you can learn from using cork is that you can improvise with lots of materials. All kinds of things can be used to make realistic terrain on your terrarium. These things can range from small pieces of wood to kitchen sponges. Be creative with your terrain making. This improvising with materials can also save you a lot of money.

Making More Complex Molds

The molds we have made so far are easy molds. All of the detail we are using is on one side of the mold. We are mounting the flat/undetailed side against the terrarium so it is not seen.

But what if you want to mold something that shows more? Maybe something like the walls that go around our medieval village as shown above. These wall units are exposed on both sides. You can see texture on this side and there is texture on the other side too. So, how do you mold something like this?

We do this in something called a two part mold. The mold is in two halves. It envelops both sides of the object to be molded. This way we can make exact copies of the whole thing.

The next picture shows you the walls. There are two different height walls and two different columns.

The wall has two heights and at intervals it has the post sections. So I will be making copies of the four different pieces shown in this picture -The short wall and short post and the tall wall and tall post.

And we need a whole bunch of each of them to go around the whole village so I will show you how to mold them and how to make lots of copies.

Let's do this process.

The first thing to do is to make your originals out of some kind of firm clay. For this I used DaVinci clay. There are many clays that are suitable including Sculpilina.

The picture shows the rough shapes cut out. From here you would go ahead and use tools to add the textures of the various rocks or bricks.

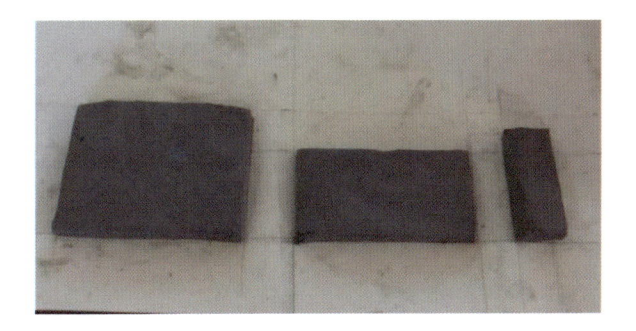

Now let's make the mold.

Make a four sided box out of cardboard, wood or foam board. Put a layer of clay in it about 2 inches thick. And embed your wall half way into it. The wall in this picture has cracked. That's ok, it adds character to the wall. And the color is lighter than the previous picture.. It has dried some which makes it stronger.

Notice how I have the bottom of the wall set right against the wall of the mold. That is the part of the wall that we won't see in the diorama. It sits on the ground. We need that against a wall of the mold because that is where we will pour the plaster into the mold. If this is unclear you will understand it clearly when you see the mold.

You can also press a couple of marbles half way into the clay . These act as registration marks that will insure the whole mold stays exactly straight. I will show you a picture of this.

Now we are going to make the first half of our mold.

Rule of Thumb*: When it comes to molding parts there is a good rule of thumb to think about. If your final product is going to be hard (like a wall) your mold should be soft and flexible like a rubber material.*

And if the final product will be rubbery and soft then you make the mold with a hard material like Plaster of Paris.

Our final product here (the wall units) is hard so we will make a rubbery mold.

For this tutorial I used a product called InstaMold. It is an easy to use product that you just mix with water and pour. But, it has a shelf life of a day or two. So, you can't set it aside and use it again like we did with the latex rubber molds we made of the cliffs earlier in this chapter.

You can also use a product called OOMOO 30 silicon mold rubber. I will show you a bit about that too.

foam board mold walls just in one corner. We still need that mold. The following picture shows me opening the mold.

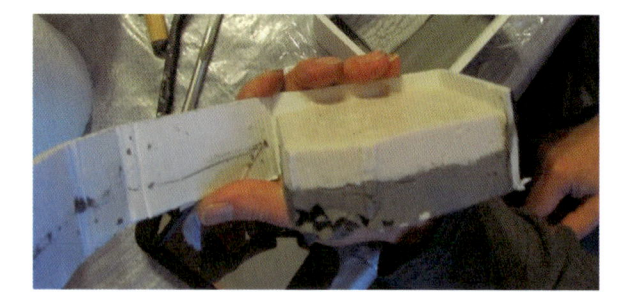

Mix up your instamold according to the directions.

TIP: If you are not sure how much mold material to make you can use the trick of pouring dry rice into your mold to fill it up. Then pour that rice into a cup. That is how much mold material you will need.

Pour the instamold right into the mold like shown here. You can see two molds that I have poured and another mold in the back getting ready for a pour.

See how half of it is clay and half of it is instamold? Our mold is half made.

Next remove all the clay but don't remove the object (wall).

This picture is not of the same wall unit as above. It is for the tower units. But this is what we now have. The clay has all been removed and we have half the instamold. And you can see the marbles in this one.

Once the Instamold has dried cut open the

Remove the marbles and rebuild the walls

of the mold right around this unit as you can see in the picture. And, coat the whole thing, mold and wall pieces with a thin coat of liquid soap. This insures the two mold halves separate cleanly. Rather than liquid soap you can use Vaseline.

Now mix up another batch of instamold and pour that right in. Once it is dried you can cut away the mold walls and discard them.

This next picture shows me removing the walls away from the completed mold.

Gently separate the two halves of the mold and remove the model or models from inside. Clean up any residue or excess clay from inside the mold and dry it a little bit with a paper towel.

Now put those two halves of the mold together and cut a couple of pieces of cardboard the same size. Put the whole assembly together with a couple of rubber bands so it all holds nicely. This picture shows you why we initially put the wall into the mold with the bottom of the wall unit against the wall of the mold. Now we can pour the plaster right into that hole.

Now mix up some plaster of paris and pour it right into the molds. Use a funnel if it makes it easier.

And there you go. Once the Plaster of Paris has dried you can take apart the mold and remove your plaster copy. Go ahead and make as many as you want. But remember that if you use Instamold the mold is only good for a day or two.

Casting In Rubber and Plastic

Okay, let's take a look at one more molding method using rubber. I show you how to make a one part rubber mold but you can use this rubber to make two part molds just like we did with these wall units.

For the medieval village we need some crates and barrels. What medieval village doesn't have crates and barrels?

The ones we make are plastic and the molds we make are rubber molds.

Just as before we start out by making our original models. With the case of the crates and barrels I used a two part epoxy called Procreate.

With Procreate you mix two halves together and then you have two hours to sculpt it until it is hardened.

Then I made quick and easy molds around the pieces by using cut pieces of paper towel tubes. I used a hot glue gun to glue down the tubes and to glue down the crate and barrel.

For this project I used a two part rubber making material from a company called Smooth-on. This is called OOMOO-30. You mix two equal parts together.

And then pour it right into your mold. Pour it in a thin stream and tap on the table a lot to get it to fill in all the little details. The tapping also will bring the bubbles up and out of the mold. You will see bubbles rise. You don't want bubbles to stick to your model. They will show up in the casting.

Once the rubber dries you can remove your model. In the case of the picture below it is the model of the barrel.

Now we can cast right into that mold.

I am going to cast little plastic barrels and crates rather than Plaster of Paris. Smooth-on also makes a two part plastic that is perfect for this. It is called OOMOO Smooth Cast 300.

You mix the two parts together and working quickly you pour it right into the mold. In a couple of minutes the plastic is set so you have to work briskly.

The next picture shows me removing the plastic crate from the mold. Now you can go ahead and make as many as you need.

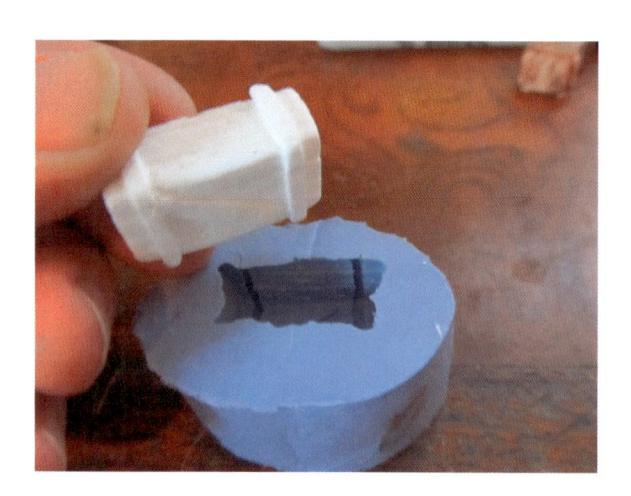

And this picture shows four copies made from one of the molds. These are the crates and one of them has been painted. They look great and are exact copies.

Making Molds

You have a whole lot of options when it comes to mold making. I have shown you a few different options and let me summarize some of the key points for you.

One Part Molds – If you have a simple object like a crate, barrel, or one side of a wall you can probably cast it in a one piece mold. To do this you can use liquid latex to brush it on like we did with the rocky outcroppings. Or you can cast the rubber like we did with the crates and barrels.

Two-Part molds – If you have a more complex object like walls with two sides or even miniature figures you want to use a two part mold like we did with the walls. In this two part mold you can use InstaMold or OOMOO rubber.

Sculpting the Models – Most of the time you can use any kind of clay. It will depend on how much detail you want. I use Davinci clay and even potters clay. If you want a really firm model with fine detail you want to use a two part epoxy clay that will harden. I use GreenStuff and ProCreate for that.

The Final Object – The material you use to cast the final object can vary. You will have great success if you use Plaster of Paris like I used for the walls. Or if you want more solid objects with more detail you can use a plastic resin like the OOMOO smooth cast I used for the crates and barrels.

The process of using ProCreate to sculpt the miniatures and OOMOO to make plastic copies is very versatile. I have used this process many times. Below you see a series of treasure chests that I made. This first picture shows the procreate model originals.

And this picture shows the plastic copes that have been painted.

Section 5

Electricity and Special Effects

Part 1: Electricity

Adding electrical functions to your diorama can take an average diorama and make it into something spectacular.

This picture shows a wizard that has a small red light bulb attached to his staff.

I accomplished this by running a pair of wires along the back of the wizard and hooking them up to a battery and a switch.

Once the wizard is mounted onto the diorama the wires are run down into it and off to the side.

There are several ways you can add this extra functionality to your diorama. In this section of the book I will cover the basics of how to wire up your diorama. In the following sections I will address the specific techniques for doing electrical special effects like lights, waterfalls, sound effects and moving parts.

Safety Warning before starting this section of the book: Electricity can be very dangerous. Always seek help from a qualified individual and these techniques should not be attempted by a child without the close supervision of an adult. Electricity, even after being brought down in voltage with a transformer can be very dangerous.

Getting Electrical Supplies

You have many options when it comes to acquiring electrical supplies for your diorama. The Scale Model Railroad industry has been making a wide variety of electrical components and parts for many decades. And the dollhouse industry makes lots of great lights, accessories and power supplies that you can use. You can also scratch build much of what you need.

The next picture shows a nice use of lighting. There is a light inside the cathedral here. And the stained glass windows are painted plastic so the light shines through nicely.

The Three Parts of a Diorama's Electrical system

When considering adding electrical function to your diorama you have to consider that there are three major parts to the system. I will describe these three parts and what they are all about.

1. The Power System
2. The Wiring
3. The Electrical parts and components

The next picture shows you my assorted parts tool box. This is a fishing tackle box that I keep all kinds of small electronic parts in. This is something you might want to do. Instead of throwing out electronic and electrical equipment that is broken or doesn't work anymore I take it apart and scavenge out various small motors, lights switches and anything else I think I might want to use. This really comes in handy.

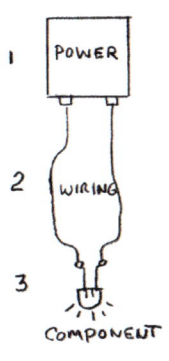

1. <u>The Power System</u> – Most model railroading, dollhouse and diorama electrical systems do not run directly on household electricity which could be rated at 110 Volts AC or more. This is much too much power and voltage for the average diorama. What these systems do is use a transformer to step the voltage down to something more practical. The image below shows a typical step down transformer. Many modern appliances such as game consoles, cell phones, telephones and other devices use these. You can often find one that will be

suitable for your diorama. The important thing to note is the output voltage. This needs to be appropriate for the electrical devices you will add to your diorama.

Typical voltage for a model railroad is 12V but it may go as high as 16V. If you want to keep things simple for your diorama you can use all model railroad equipment. The industry makes a wide variety of lights and other apparatus that is all pretty much standardized.

If you are going to improvise your own wiring then you should select the components you are going to use first, then choose a power supply that meets the demands. For example, if you are going to use a series of LED's (Light emitting diodes) that require 5 volts to operate then you would find and use a step down transformer or some kind of power supply with a 5 volt DC output.

Power Supply

I use a nice little hobby power supply. It is shown in the next picture. You plug it into your wall outlet and the output shown as the red and black knobs, is variable. You can vary the voltage between 0 and 15 volts. You can buy something like this for around twenty-five dollars.

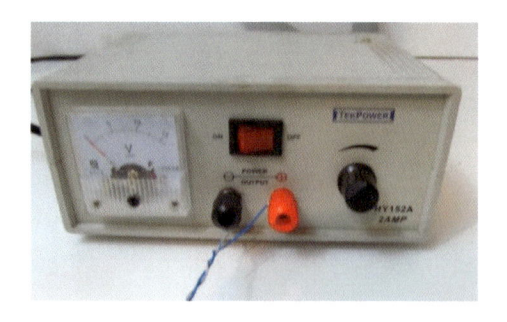

Batteries as an alternate plan

If your wiring requirements are not complex, say you only want to have one or two small lights you can go with a battery system. This is easily accomplished with a battery holder like the one in the picture below. This one holds 4 1.5 volt AA batteries. You can purchase these at hobby shops, radio shack or you can even remove them from various electronic toys.

You can also wire up a simple 9 volt system with a 9 volt battery and case.

Remove the battery plug from an old piece of electronics like a toy or a transistor radio. You can also buy these plugs.

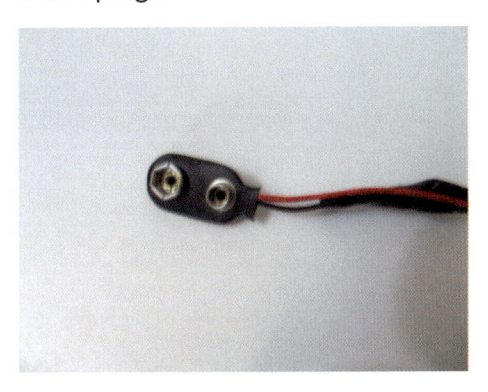

2. <u>The wiring</u> – This is the series of wires that you put in your diorama to bring the power from the power supply to the various parts and components on your diorama. Typically you have to run two wires for each component. Wire is measured in Gauges and there are a lot of different size gauges you can use. A common and easy to find wire you can use is telephone or bell wire. This comes in a sheath with either two or four separate wires in it.

3. <u>The parts and components</u> – While this is the third thing we are taking a look at it is the most important. You have to decide first which components such as lights, pumps, waterfalls and motors that you want on your diorama and where you will install them. From this you can decide which power supply you need and where you can run the wires.

Basic Electrical Theory

There is a bit of basic electrical theory you should know when considering adding electricity to your diorama. Here is an overview.

There are two major types of electrical supply and they are AC and DC. These stand for alternating current and Direct current. And this distinction could be important. It all depends on the components you are going to mount into your diorama. Some electrical components require AC or DC and you have to make sure you get the right supply. Other components like simple light bulbs will work on either AC or DC.

Every component you use will need to have two wires going to it. This is important to remember when you are building the diorama. The electricity needs to go to the component on one wire and return back to the power supply on the other wire. This is a closed loop.

The next illustration is a typical simple electrical theory circuit. It shows the two wires going from the power supply to the component and it also shows the switch that is installed to turn the light on and off. Think of the wires as pipes that electricity flows through. The switch will open the pipe and stop the flow.

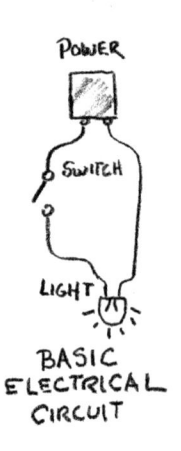

BASIC ELECTRICAL CIRCUIT

You can see in the example above that when the switch is open no electricity will flow. This is important to consider when you have multiple components in your diorama because if a component should go bad or blowout it can affect the other components by opening up the circuit and not allowing electricity to flow to them.

You avoid this by wiring all the components in parallel.

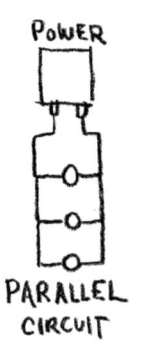

PARALLEL CIRCUIT

What this means is that each component has two wires running to the power supply. The illustration below shows this arrangement with three light bulbs.

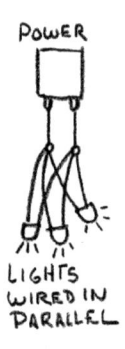

LIGHTS WIRED IN PARALLEL

This wiring in parallel gives you a lot of flexibility in how you control these lights and components. For example you can have one switch that turns everything on and off or you can have separate switches that operate each individual light.

The picture below shows three lights with a single main on and off switch that turns them all on or off.

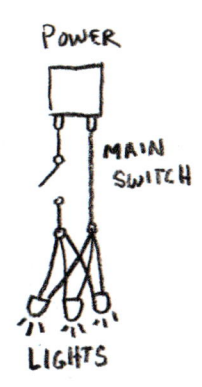

The picture below shows how, with parallel wiring, you can put separate switches in to operate the various components and lights individually.

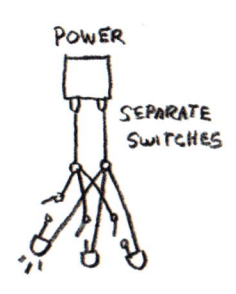

Pre wiring your Diorama

Before you start building your diorama you should figure out what kind of electrical components you are going to have in it and where they will go. This is so you can do some of the wiring work before the diorama is complete.

The next picture shows a shadowbox style diorama that is made with foam. You can see that I have run the wires in the early stage of the diorama making process.

Drill holes and cut out runways wherever you need the wires to go. And remember to run two wires for every component.

You can do some drilling and cutting when the diorama is done but doing as much of the wiring as possible as early as possible is advantageous and will look better. You can hide all the wiring behind the various terrain features.

As you are designing your diorama on paper you should make notations where the various electrical components will go so you can add these wires as you are building.

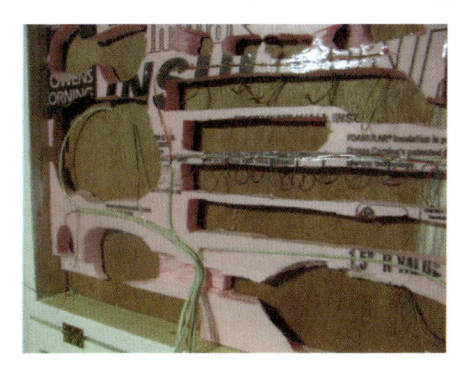

The next picture shows the 300 diorama nearly completed. Inside each of the mountain peaks there is a speaker mounted. You have to install those speakers early in the process of making the diorama. I installed them while it was still a cardboard frame. With a large component like a speaker it really is a good idea to get it installed and wired as soon as possible. Otherwise you would have to cut and repair the terrain in your diorama.

So plan out the electronics and electricity of your diorama as early as possible and do as much of the wiring in the early stages.

Using an Electronics Project Box

If you are doing a large diorama or one with a lot of electrical components you can wire them all into an electronics project box. This is an empty plastic box that is made for the purpose. You can drill out holes and install switches and lights. It becomes a sort of control panel for your diorama. Electronics supply stores like Radio Shack carry these.

LIGHTS IN YOUR DIORAMA

You have a lot of choices when it comes to lights in your diorama. The bulbs in the picture at left shows a standard hobby bulb that operates on 1.5 volts. This type of bulb has been used by hobbyists for a very long time and there are a lot of options for using it. You can get screw in sockets for it. These are reasonably durable and easy to replace when they burn out and you can get them in a variety of different voltages. And generally they will work with both AC and DC power.

This type of bulb is the simplest and easiest route you can go but they do take up a lot of power so if you are using batteries you should take this into consideration and switch to LED's if you want longer battery life.

Christmas Bulbs

One of my favorite types of bulb is the Christmas tree bulbs. They come in a long string with lots of little bulbs. Typically you can just cut out a lamp and it works on low voltage.

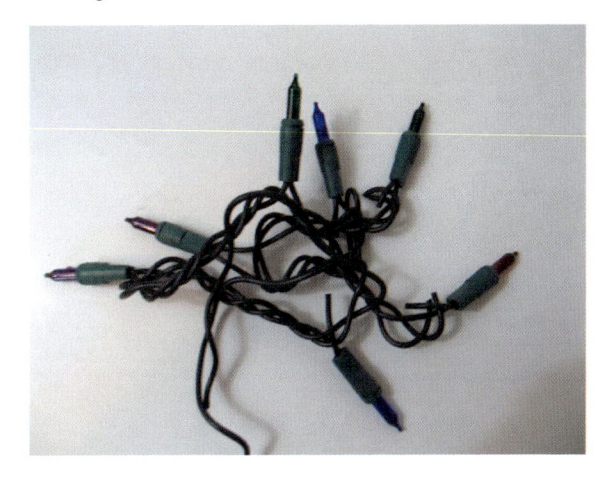

More Bulb Options

You can buy packs of small bulbs at Radio Shack. These shown here are mini colored lamps and they work on 6v.

This next picture shows how I removed one of the bulbs from the string and wired it up to stand alone.

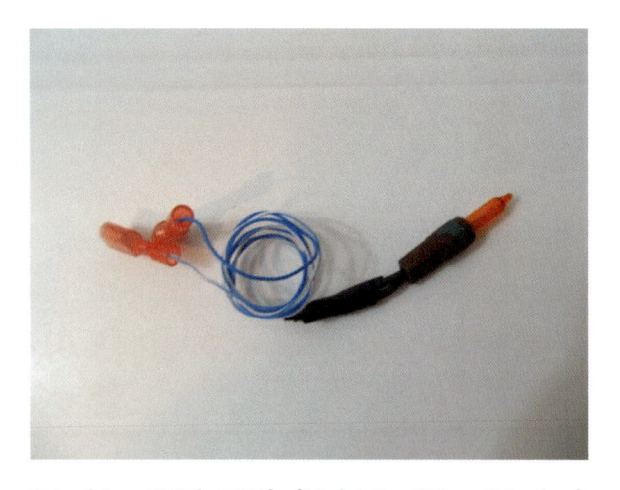

Working With LED's (Light Emitting Diodes)

LED's are an excellent way to add light to your diorama. They are inexpensive and easy to install. There are just a few rules you have to know when working with them. I will go over some of these basics.

LED's are polarized devices. This means that they can only work on DC voltage. They have a plus side (+) and a minus side (-) and you have to connect them to your battery or power supply in this correct way. The plus side on the LED is always the longer lead. If you look at the previous picture showing the red LED alongside the penny you can see that one of the wire leads is longer than the other. This is the lead that you hook up to the plus side (+) of your power source. This is an industry standard and all LED's are made this way.

The Voltage of LED's

They do vary in how much voltage they need to operate correctly and you have to make sure you apply the correct voltage. Typically this is around 5 volts but it does vary.

Limiting the current to the LED

One important thing to note about LED's is that they are very sensitive to the amount of electricity that flows through them. If you hook one up directly to a power source, even if the voltage is correct the LED will probably be damaged and stop working; this is because they offer very little resistance to current flow and easily get overloaded and burn out.

We prevent this by adding a small resistor in series with the LED. This is typically 200 ohms as a minimum. This will control and limit the amount of electrical current that flows.

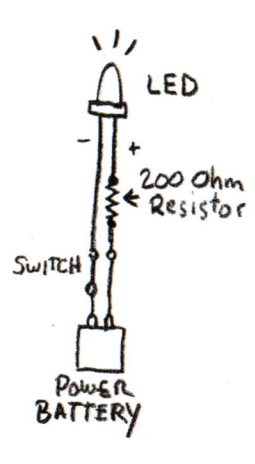

Each LED that you install should have one of these resistors.

Various LED's

One of the great things about LED's is that they come in a very wide assortment of sizes, voltages and performance types.

You can get them in just about any color and you can get them in various sizes. You can also get LED's that blink which is a nice option.

Here is a picture of an LED in action. That is a little foam blacksmith forge with a red LED.

Part 2: Special Effects

Waterfalls

Adding a working waterfall to your diorama can bring it to new levels of interest and excitement. And you can do it relatively cheaply. One of the best things you can do is find an inexpensive table top waterfall and remove all the relevant parts from it and use it in your diorama.

You can also purchase a waterfall pump and install it into your diorama. The picture below shows from left to right the transformer to power the pump, the switch unit to turn it on and off and the actual pump unit with a short hose.

Here is the basic design of how a pump works. Small pumps typically sit right in the water reservoir and suck the water from their underside. So you sit the pump right in the hidden reservoir. In this case the hidden reservoir is underneath a mountain.

The pump draws water and sends it up the hose to an opening in the side of the mountain. The water acts as a waterfall and makes its way down to another reservoir. This is a small pond right in the diorama. From this small pond the water drains back down by gravity into the pump reservoir.

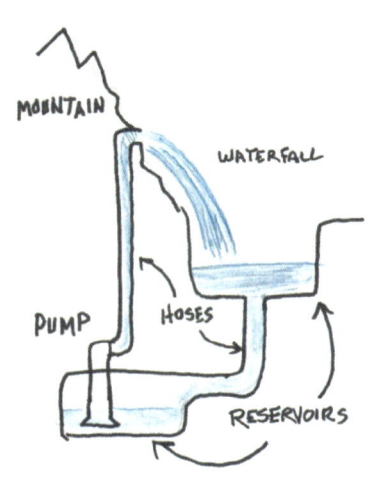

Typically it is best to hide the pump and all of its apparatus in this manner. All you want to see is the waterfall and the miniature pond.

Things to watch for when getting a pump

A lot of these small pumps have either an adjustment dial or adjustment ring so you can control the flow of the water. This comes in handy to make sure you get the right amount of flow. Ideally you want the pond to be always full but yet still draining into the lower reservoir.

The height of the water being raised

Pumps do not raise water to an infinite height. They will only raise it up to a certain height depending on the power of the particular pump. Make sure you get a pump that will raise water high enough for your diorama application. This is measured in inches of lift. So measure in inches how high you need the water to be pumped and get a pump that can handle it.

Web Resource: You can see more of this diorama and see a video of the waterfall in action on my website here:

http://www.stormthecastle.com/diorama/diorama-video-medieval-castle.htm

Water Proofing Your Terrain

Of course if you are going to put any kind of real water in your diorama you are going to have to waterproof the terrain. I recommend you do this in several coats and some of the materials you can use are either Realistic water by Woodland Scenics or Clear Casting Resin which is a two part mix. You mix together then brush or pour it on . Use of these products will seal the surface of the diorama so it won't be affected by water. Make sure you test it in small amounts to verify you didn't miss any spots. And I recommend you always do more than one coat.

Alternative Sealant: You can also use

polyurethane. This is sold in hardware stores and it is typically used to waterseal furniture, decks and other wooden things. It does work well but you should do multiple coats.

Automation and Moving Parts

Adding automation and moving parts to a diorama can take it to levels that dioramas rarely achieve. But it does take a little bit of work and some skill to accomplish this.

There are plenty of small motors that you can readily adapt to your diorama though. I have a large collection that I use in my dioramas.

You can buy small motors from hobby stores and electronic stores. You can also harvest them from old pieces of electronics that are broken or no longer needed. Good examples of this are VCR's and cassette players.

Where to buy cheap motors and automation parts?

Here are a couple of companies that have lots of great little electronics and motors that can be used by hobbyists:

- American Science & Surplus – www.sciplus.com
- Edmund Scientifics - www.scientificsonline.com

When harvesting various electronic parts like motors from old appliances it is important to think about the usefulness of other items too. For example, along with a motor you might want to take any pulleys, gears and belts. This is so you can make the drive systems that go along with the motor. You have to attach the motor to parts in your diorama somehow.

A look at a motorized drawbridge

Servos –

A servo is a great little electronic device that is used in Radio controlled toys like airplanes and cars. Think of a radio controlled car and how when you turn the wheel on the hand held unit the wheels on the car actually turn. This is done by something called a servo and you really don't have to worry about the radio controlled aspect of it. What you really want to use is the little motor or "servo" that does the work.

A servo is a powerful little motorized unit that will give you a controlled amount of motion. All you have to do is vary the voltage to it.

The picture below shows a servo that is

being used to open a drawbridge on a castle diorama. A servo is perfect for this application because it has good strength, moves at a relatively slow rate and you can move it through as much motion as you want. In other words it doesn't just rotate like a motor. It rotates as much as you want it to. Just like the steering on an RC car.

There are lots of different sizes and types of servos but they pretty much all do the same thing and there are two things for you to take care of when using one of these. It needs some kind of a controller and some kind of power supply.

Both of these issues can easily be solved. You can buy something called a "servo driver" which is a little electronic device with a knob on it. You plug the servo into it and you can turn the knob to turn the servo. And for the power supply you can either use some kind of power supply or even use a battery for an RC plane or car. This kind of battery is designed to run servos.

The picture below shows a setup for the servo. The servo itself is on the right. On the left is the battery and in the center is the yellow servo driver. You turn the knob on the driver and the servo moves accordingly.

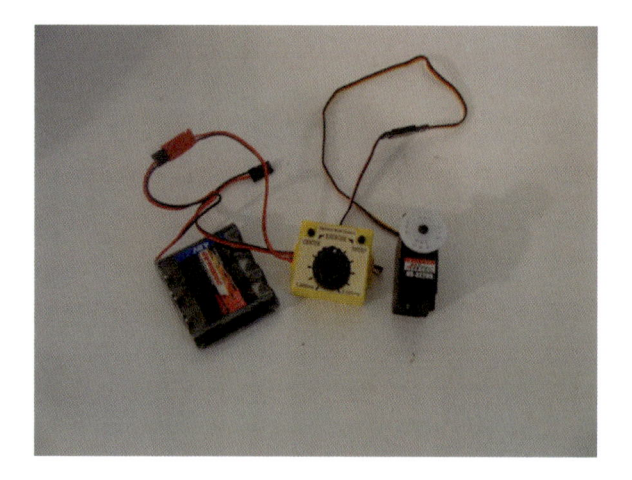

Something like this is inexpensive and can add some terrific special effects to your diorama. It is just a matter of running the wires and hooking up the servo in a way so that it moves the desired object. In the case of my drawbridge you can see in the picture that I just hot glued the arm of the servo right to the drawbridge. It will be real easy to camouflage it with some wood or terrain materials.

Small motors and

gears

You have a lot of creative things you can do with small motors and you can even use one from an old clock. The typical challenges apply where you have to connect it to your diorama in some way and you have to provide it with power. If you buy a small motor you should get the power requirements with it and often times motors will be labeled with their power needs including AC, DC and level of voltage required.

Getting a small variable power supply

You can purchase a small desktop power supply that is usually more than adequate for all your automation needs. Typically they will put out voltages between 1 and 15volts which is enough to power most small motors and lights. And because they are variable you can use them for a wide assortment of parts that have different voltage requirements. So whether your small dc motor needs 5 volts or 10 volts you can power it up.

The following picture shows a little motor and gear setup that I took out of a tape recorder. It is nicely setup for me to add a string and power an elevator on a string.

Being a dc motor if you hook up the voltage one way it goes up and if you reverse the polarity it goes in the opposite direction. So I used a three pole switch and the elevator goes up and down depending on which way I switch it.

The drawing below shows the wiring of a double pole double throw switch. This is how the polarity is easily reversed with the throw of a switch and the motor is reversed. The dashed line is the switch housing.

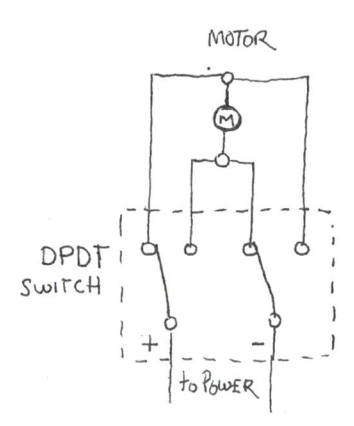

When it comes to automation in a diorama the possibilities are endless. This picture shows a flour mill that has a little motor in it. The wheel slowly turns.

It has this six volt motorized gearbox inside. This gearbox is ready made. I bought it for twelve dollars. I used hardening clay to connect the wooden dowel shaft to it. The Mill wheel attaches to that shaft. In the picture you can see the gearbox is attached to a piece of foam board. This will go right into the building.

Section 6

Buildings and Structures

Some Medieval structures

In this section I will take you through a variety of building techniques.

Basic Building structures

The Picture below shows three medieval buildings. Some of the techniques I will cover include the basic shape of the buildings, the woodwork, plastering, the thatched roof and stonework.

The shell of the building can be made out of any one of several different materials. I use foam board because it is durable, fairly waterproof, and easy to work with.

The following picture shows the basic structure of a foam board building. I cut out all the individual pieces then used a hot glue gun to glue them together.

Start out with paper or card stock

I do recommend that you first make your buildings out of card stock or heavy card paper. This will allow you to easily modify and change it. You will also be able to visualize the scale of it.

Once you have it made out of card paper then you can trace the patterns of the walls onto foam board.

The door and window holes are optional. Sometimes its ok to just paint the spaces for them black or dark brown. The option is yours. I like to cut out the doors and windows and then I can install doors that are recessed. It gives a better look.

Once you have the structure all built you can coat the building with grout or Celluclay. Grout is a building material you can buy at any hardware store. Use the unsanded grout. It is easier to work with. And Celluclay gives a wonderful texture but it is a bit more coarse and gives a grittier look.

I use grout for standard medieval buildings and I use celluclay for fortresses with a rougher look.

It is a bit difficult to see but in the last picture I have already grouted the building.

Next you cut thin strips of balsa wood and apply them in various patterns to the building. It is better looking if you paint them first.

Generally the thinner the balsa wood the better. The width of them will change depending on the size and shape of your building.

A tacky glue works best for this. Hot Glue Gun will not adhere to the grout very well. Just outline the corners of the building, the doors, and the windows.

After this it is just a matter of painting the walls and the timbers. I typically paint the walls an antique white which is a bit different than a plain white.

There are a couple more details about this building that I want to show you.

After the roof was fully applied I then painted it with a clear sealant This gives it a more straw like look. And while the sealant was still wet I used a variety of sharp tools to create a grainy look. You can also use a wire brush to get the nap to all go in the right direction.

The Base of the building looks like stone work. This is just a flat piece of foam that I laid down then set the building on. And the chimney is also just a piece of foam glued to the roof.

And the most impressive thing about this building is the thatched roof. I cut strips of bath towel and glued them in succession to the roof starting on each side and working toward the top in overlapping layers.

The Light

I also created a lamp on wires and glued that into the building. Now we will be able to light up the inside of the building.

Let's take a look at another building

This is a medieval tower and it uses many of the techniques we have already looked at including being built out of foam board, having the balsa wood framing, and being coated in grout. But there are a few different techniques here that I can show you. These are the shingled roof and the cast stone wall.

Making an Easy Shingled Roof

You can also do a shingled look on the roofs of buildings. The best ways to do this would be to make small shingles out of balsa wood and glue them in succession to the roof. This is very labor intensive though and you can cheat a bit by creating the roof slabs out of balsa wood and then using tools to scratch out a shingled look as shown in the picture below.

Painting and Washing the Roof

But in order for this technique you have to be a bit careful about how you paint it. First you paint the whole thing with a gray paint. Then once the paint is almost dry you do a technique called "washing". This is where you paint it with a very wet black paint. This causes the black to run into the various cracks and lines. Once you have washed it you immediately wipe it with a dry paper towel. You end up with most of the roof being gray but the black stays embedded in the cracks.

You can try different colors for this type of roof and shades of red/orange also work very well. They make it look like a clay roof.

Making the Stone Wall

This picture shows a close-up of the stone wall that goes all the way around the building.

This technique takes some work and some casting. I will show you how to make this.

We are going to make a rubber mold that we can use to pour Plaster of Paris into. When you make a rubber mold one of the big advantages is that you can use it over and over again to cast as many stone walls as you want. In the case of this tower I have cast four of these so I can use one for each wall.

Making a Mold

You start out by laying out a thin sheet of clay on a table. Then you press stones into it. Arrange it all so it looks like a stone wall. Be sure to press the clay around the stones so there are no large gaps. I just used a random number of pebbles with interesting shapes. This particular mold I am making is about eight inches square.

Once you have the model wall the way you want it you have to paint it with some kind of a sealant. I used a painters sealant that is brushed on. You can buy a sealant in any arts and crafts store.

Once the sealant has dried we can cast a latex rubber mold over it.

Latex rubber can be bought from a variety of companies including Woodland Scenics and I used a product called "Mold Maker". This type of latex is a thick liquid that air dries once you start using it.

You simply brush it right onto the model in thin layers allowing it to dry between layers. Typically you want to do at least 5-6 layers of the latex so the mold will be strong and durable. And if you want the mold to be extra strong you can even put down a layer of cheese cloth or bandage cloth then apply several more layers of latex.

The picture below shows my clay and pebble model covered in Latex.

Once the latex has dried you can carefully peel it off the clay wall. You now have a perfect negative image of your wall. You can cast plaster of paris into it to make all the stone walls you need.

Once the Plaster of Paris dries you can gently remove it from the mold and make more of them. The picture below shows the rubber mold and a couple of stone walls that have been cast in it.

From here it is just a matter of cutting the walls to the size needed and painting them.

The Painting then washing technique works very well on stone walls. This is the same technique that we used for the shingled roof. It gives an overall gray color then the black settles in to the cracks between the stones in the wall.

Some Casting Tips

Just about any clay will work for this and I use DaVinci Clay because it is easy to shape and never dries out.

And if you are using clay you always have to seal it with some kind of a sealant. Otherwise it will stick to the latex and possibly ruin the look of it. As a minimum the clay wall you made will be ruined.

Other things – This technique of embedding small stones in clay is just one way to make a stone wall. You have lots of other options and you can experiment. For example, if you wanted a brick wall you could lay down uniform sheet of clay and rather than pressing pebbles into it you could sculpt out the lines of bricks with a sharp instrument. Seal it then make a mold of it and voila you have a brick wall.

Mold release – There is a product called mold release. This is a liquid that you spray into the mold and it will prevent the latex from sticking to your model. It makes separation much easier.

You can even use a spray bottle to very lightly mist the model with water before applying the latex. This also works pretty good as a mold release.

Now you cut the Plaster of Paris wall with a saw or sharp knife and you can glue it to the building.

Having a mold like this is very versatile and you can use this stone wall for buildings, towers, walls, bridges, wells or just about anything else that has a roughhewn stone wall.

Some more roof techniques

In this section I will show you three more roof making techniques.

I have shown you how to make a nice roof out of some cloth but you can also use other techniques to make roofs including casting them in plaster.

We do this by first making an original out of clay. The picture below shows a thatched roof that is formed out of clay. I used a square of wood that I notched to impress the shingle look on a sheet of clay.

Then I built a box around the clay and poured a mold making material into it. In this case I used something called InstaMold. It works really well and dries quickly. In half an hour you can separate the mold from the original.

This picture shows the wooden structure to make around the model. I sealed it with hot glue gun so the instamold wouldn't run out.

You pour in the instamold and let it dry.

Once it has dried you can gently separate the mold from the clay model. Now you can cast plaster of paris into the mold and make lots of roofs.

Alternatives – I used Instamold because you just add water and it is pretty easy to use. You can also use latex rubber. Or any one of the many other mold making materials.

Note when making molds – The biggest problem you will come across when making molds is little air bubbles that will cling to the model and show up in the mold distorting the final product.

This picture shows what the air bubbles do to the cast piece.

You can minimize the air bubbles by knocking on the table sharply several times. This loosens the air bubbles and brings them to the top and out of the rubber. You do knocking this immediately after you pour the instamold.

Clay Shingled roof

You can experiment with this technique of making molds of roofs and another style that looks great is the clay shingle. The picture shows this type of shingle. This one is half painted.

I created this mold by laying out a layer of clay then using a wooden dowel (1/4" thick) to impress the shingle shapes. Just lay in rows of them.

The following picture shows a clay shingled roof model.

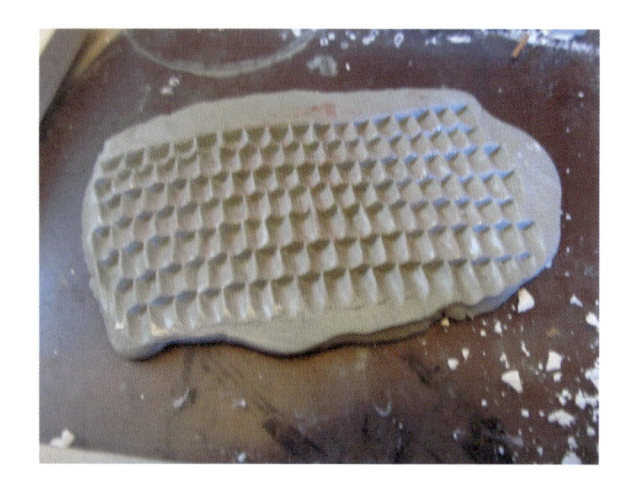

Wood Thatched Roof

The final technique for roof making is an easy one but it looks absolutely fantastic. This is where you cut small pieces of balsa wood or basswood and add them to the roof like shingles – one at a time. It takes some time but it is worth it.

Here is what it looks like finished. You should use a fast setting glue with a lot of tack to do something like this. I use a hot glue gun.

One thing to note about this is that because the shingles are embedded down you can't make the regular mold. It would be backwards. The shingles would indent rather than stick out. So, I coated this clay model with a sealant and cast the plaster of paris right onto it.

A Castle Tower out of foam

Ok, in this section we will cover one more structure building technique. In an earlier chapter we looked at how foam was great for dioramas. And I showed you a little bit about that. But foam is also terrific for the buildings themselves.

So here is a look at how to use foam to make a castle structure. You can use this to make all kinds of fortress like buildings and even whole castle setups.

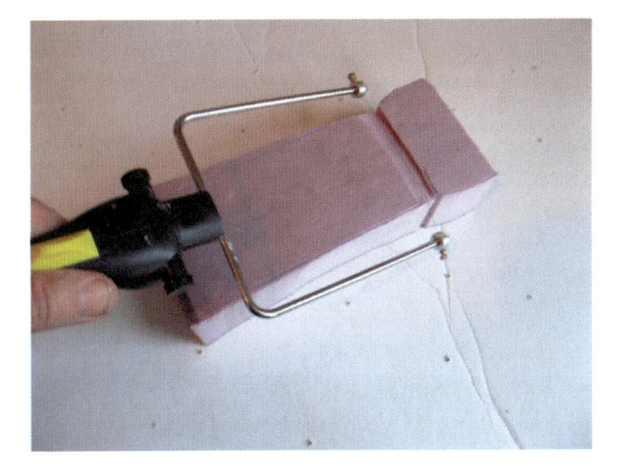

I uses a hot wire foam cutter to shape out a medieval tower.

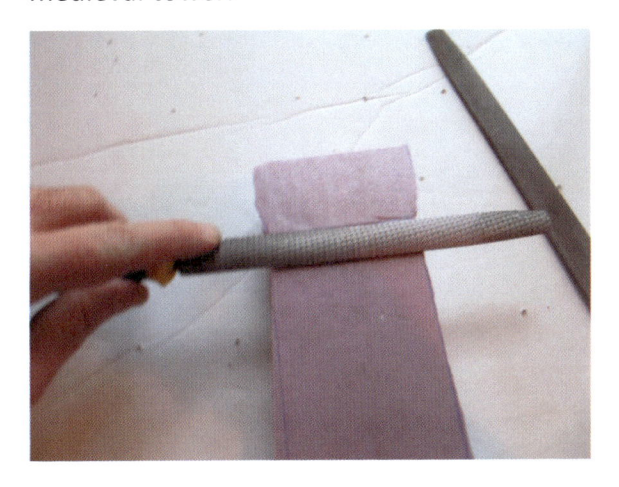

You can use a wide variety of tools to shape it including files, rasps, and sandpaper.

Notice the window and the door. These are all sculpted with the tools. Next put in the brick shapes with a pencil or pen.

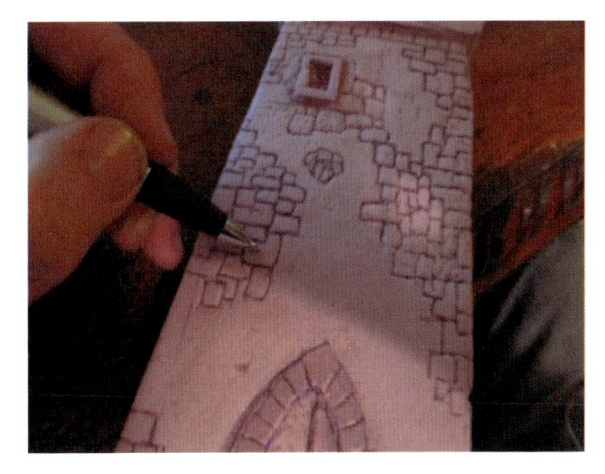

The only thing remaining is to paint it. But we will save that for the very next chapter on painting tips.

Section 7
Painting Techniques

Painting is of course a very important part of diorama work and I am going to show you a few basic techniques here .

The Basic Painting Technique

When painting something like the walls of the buildings or the roof there are three steps that you take. This is a technique that you can use in a lot of different applications.

1. You paint the base color
2. You use a washing technique to add black into the cracks and crevices
3. You use a dry brushing technique to add highlights to the item.

First choose your base color and paint the whole item. You can be liberal with the paint and an uneven coat with darker and lighter sections is usually best. I have painted part of this roof with a poppy orange color.

Let's finish off the painting of the medieval tower. It will really show how the three steps of base paint, wash, and highlighting works and looks.

First the gray/stone is painted on. Then it is allowed to dry.

Then you use a very wet paintbrush with just a little black and you wash over the whole thing. The black will run into the cracks and crevices. This is great. Use lots of water and spread it around.

Second the black wash is applied.

Finally you use a lighter shade of your base color. I mix a little white with the poppy orange and you brush this onto the high portions of the object. Do not add water to this color. Use the raw color right out of the tube.

Finally the white highlights are applied. You do this by getting paint on the brush then brushing most of it off so the brush is pretty dry. Then you lightly brush over the surface of the tower.

And the Tower is complete.

Let's take one more look at using foam and doing some of the detail paint.

Here is a foam castle structure and we want a nice clay shingled roof on it. You can draw out the pattern of the roof tiles with a pen, slowly scoring the foam with deeper and deeper marks. Then wash in a layer of wet black. You can then wipe it with a cloth to clean off all the tops.

Then dry brush a layer of red over it.

It looks great!

Section 8

Unique and Interesting diorama housings

When it comes to making dioramas we often think about how to make the scene as realistic as possible and this is great, even with a fantasy diorama. But, often times we don't think about the overall size, shape and theme of the diorama in terms of how it is housed.

This is something you might want to give some thought to because it opens up a whole new world in the art of diorama making.

In this section I will show you a few unique diorama housings.

The Cigar box Diorama

Cigar boxes make wonderful little diorama containers. And they are very cheap to get. You can often get a few for free.

And this diorama makes use of the inside of the box and the inside lid of the box.

The Diorama Inside a Light bulb

This was a fun little project where I built a castle with lots of towers right inside a light bulb. It actually has a little actuator switch inside it so you can put a magnet near it and light up the castle.

I don't show you how to make this. I just wanted to show you a neat diorama housing.

The Magic Mirror Illusion Diorama

This is a small hand-held diorama that you pick up and then look into the eye hole.

The box itself is only about a foot long. But when looking inside you see an object that is two feet away. I do this with a mirror.

This next picture shows you inside the diorama. The eyehole is on the left. You look into it and the light path bounces off the two mirrors on the right. The object you see is on the bottom left of the diorama.

The Wall Diorama

Here is the wall diorama mounted on the wall. This is a lot of fun and people love to look at it while operating the various controls.

I used an old wooden window frame and made a box for it to mount on the wall.

Here is a closer look:

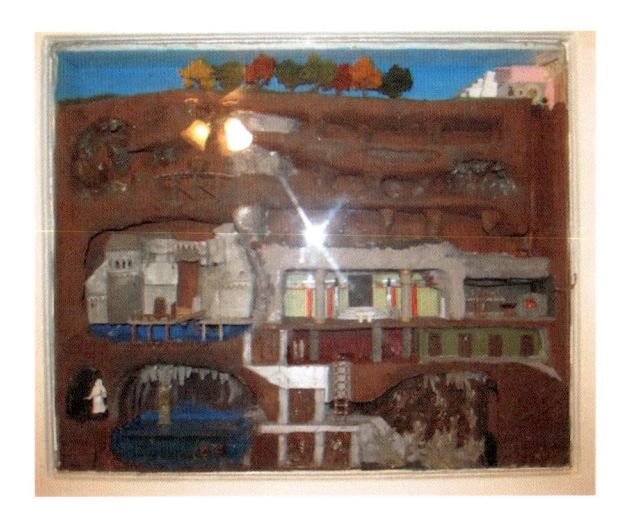

ABOUT THE AUTHOR

Will Kalif is a webmaster and writer. He has published several books on a wide variety of subjects including dioramas and mead making. You can learn more about Will and his dioramas by visiting his website at www.stormthecastle.com

Printed in Poland
by Amazon Fulfillment
Poland Sp. z o.o., Wrocław